VOLUME**THREE**

GYPSY**JAZZ**GUITAR
SOLOINGETUDES

Learn Guitar Soloing Strategies & Techniques For 6 Essential Gypsy Jazz Standards

REMI**HARRIS**

FUNDAMENTAL**CHANGES**

Gypsy Jazz Guitar Soloing Etudes – Volume Three

Learn Guitar Soloing Strategies & Techniques For 6 Essential Gypsy Jazz Standards

ISBN: 978-1-78933-456-2

Published by **www.fundamental-changes.com**

Copyright © 2025 Remi Harris

Edited by Tim Pettingale

www.fundamental-changes.com

Join our free Facebook Community of Cool Musicians

www.facebook.com/groups/fundamentalguitar

Instagram: **FundamentalChanges**

For over 350 Free Guitar Lessons with Videos Check Out

www.fundamental-changes.com

Cover Image Copyright: Shutterstock, krsmanovic

Contents

Introduction

Welcome to Volume Three of *Gypsy Jazz Guitar Etudes*. This series is dedicated to helping you learn the language of Gypsy Jazz guitar.

Like any language, learning how to speak the vocabulary of Gypsy Jazz is best achieved through conversation rather than reading a dictionary. In my first book for Fundamental Changes, *100 Gypsy Jazz Licks for Guitar*, we learned dozens of authentic licks that can be played over static chords, and over the major and minor II V I sequences, which crop up frequently in this music.

In this series, we take things a step further by learning how to improvise over actual tunes from the Gypsy repertoire, while working on the important skill of constructing a solo.

It's important to have something to say over your favourite tunes and to have strategies for navigating the chord changes, and that's what these books are all about. Throughout the course of the series you'll learn to solo over the all-time great Gypsy Jazz standards, plus a number of jazz standards that have found their way into the Gypsy Jazz repertoire.

For each of these etudes, I played a solo over a few choruses of the changes. Each solo is then broken down into chunks and explained in detail. Each musical example represents a complete idea (i.e., a lick over a few bars that has a clear beginning, middle and end). This means that when you come to the difficult bridge section of a popular tune, for example, you'll have a something ideal to play over it, plus an explanation of why it works. Over time, you'll not only add to your library of licks, you'll grow your understanding of the harmony of this music too.

I hope you have fun with it!

Remi

Get the Audio & Video

The audio files for this book are available to download for free from **www.fundamental-changes.com.** The link is in the top right-hand corner. Click on the "Guitar" link then simply select this book title from the drop-down menu and follow the instructions to get the audio.

We recommend that you download the files directly to your computer (not to your tablet or phone) and extract them there before adding them to your media library. If you encounter any difficulty, we provide technical support within 24 hours via the contact form.

For over 350 free guitar lessons with videos check out:

www.fundamental-changes.com

Join our free Facebook Community of Cool Musicians

www.facebook.com/groups/fundamentalguitar

Tag us for a share on Instagram: **FundamentalChanges**

Get the Video:

A performance video of every full solo in this book is available at:

https://geni.us/gypsythree

Or scan the QR code below:

An Overview of My Approach

In my first book, *100 Gypsy Jazz Guitar Licks*, I explained my approach to improvising over chord changes in some detail. Here, I'll give just a brief overview of my approach, so you can understand how I think when presented with a set of chord changes, and learn the simple concept I use to create lines.

Whenever I post videos online, the question I'm most often asked is, "What scale did you use to play that line?" It might surprise you to know that scales are not usually my primary thought when I'm playing.

When I compose or improvise licks, I generally think in terms of chord tones and chord movements. I may play ideas that are scale-based from time to time, but my main focus is on the individual chord tones and how they relate to the root note of the chord and/or the home key of the chord sequence.

A good way to start thinking like this is to focus on specific chord shapes, the chord tones that make up those shapes, and the other chord tones that are located nearby.

First, we need to visualise a chord shape and think of all its notes in relation to the *root note* of that chord. Let's say it's a Dm7 chord. We could choose to base our melodic ideas around this common shape below.

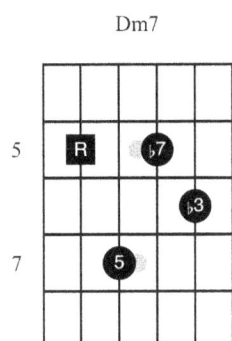

The chord tones illustrated above are the strong notes of the chord – the root, b3, 5th and b7. These are all *safe* notes we can rest on and create melodies with.

But all the notes that surround the chord tones are available to use when soloing too. Each plays a slightly different role and will create a different sound in relation to the chord.

The diagram below shows *all* the potential passing notes in easy reach of the chord shape, beginning on the fifth string where the root is located.

Dm7

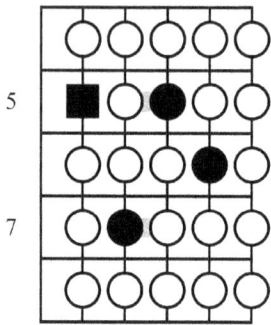

Of course, on its own, this diagram looks very intimidating! So, let's break it down.

We can split these passing notes into two groups:

1. Repeated chord tones/extended notes

2. Chromatic notes

First, some of these notes will just be repeated chord tones, while others will be extended tones. This is shown in the grid below. Within this shape are repeats of the root, b3, 5th and b7. Then we have the 6th, 9th and 11th extended tones. These extensions will add a different colour to the sound of the basic Dm7 without going outside the harmony.

Dm7

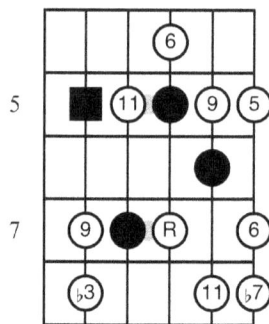

Here's a simple lick based on the above shape that uses a combination of chord tones and extended notes. It ends on the G (11th) note on the second string to create a Dm11 sound.

Chord visualisation exercise 1

So, the first way in which we can invent a lick around a chord shape is to understand where the chord tones and extensions are located in relation to the root note.

The second group of passing notes – those that are neither chord tones nor extensions – are *chromatic* notes i.e., they don't belong to the parent chord. The diagram below shows the chromatic note options in relation to the root of the chord.

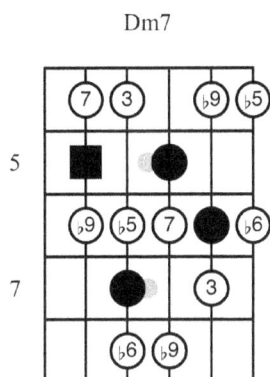

Extensions like the 6th, 9th and 11th are not too far away from the basic chord tones, so we can rest on those notes and they will create a different colour of minor chord.

Others, like the b5, b9, or the use of the major 3rd over a chord that has a minor 3rd, create a sound much further away from the basic tones, so we tend not to rest on these notes unless we are going for a more outside or altered sound. However, they are still useful as passing notes to create tension and release. We can use them to *target* the strong chord tones and extensions.

When we combine these two sets of colours, we can compose licks that weave in and out of the harmony creating tension and release. Work through this longer lick and identify which extended and chromatic notes I've used to embellish the basic Dm7 chord shape.

Chord visualisation exercise 2

Now have a go at creating a couple of licks of your own around this chord shape.

- First, compose a line that uses only chord tones and extensions

- Next, introduce some chromatic passing notes

A great tip here is to aim to play chord tones/extended notes mostly on down-beats and chromatic passing notes mostly on up-beats. If you play chord tones on the strong beats of the bar most of the time, your licks will sound grounded, no matter how many chromatic embellishments you add.

This idea can be applied to any chord shape you know.

In the chapters that follow, I'll point out all the chord shapes I had in mind when I played a specific lick, so you can see how the idea originated. Then you can experiment with that shape and see what ideas of your own you can invent.

If this concept is new to you and you'd like to dig deeper into it, check out *100 Gypsy Jazz Guitar Licks*, published by Fundamental Changes.

Chapter One – 12-Bar Blues in Bb

To play authentic jazz, it always helps to have played and studied the blues, because jazz ultimately has its roots in the blues. Good phrasing is a very important part of blues soloing, with its call and response and vocal-like approach, so having a good working knowledge of the genre will immediately improve your jazz vocabulary.

Bb is a common key for the blues in the jazz genre. In 1938 Django Reinhardt recorded *Blue Light Blues* with Benny Carter and his orchestra and, circa 1947, *Django's Blues* – both blues in Bb. Other Bb blues jazz standards that have found their way into the Gypsy Jazz repertoire include Sonny Rollin's *Sonny Moon for Two* and *Tenor Madness*.

For each example in this and subsequent chapters, I'll suggest some chord shapes around which the melodic lines can be built. As mentioned in the introduction, when I solo, I think in terms of chord tones and chord movements. To develop this melodic approach requires being able to visualise chord shapes in different areas of the fretboard. To work on this skill, for each example I suggest holding down the chords and looking at where the notes of the solo are located around it. This way you'll begin to build a solid connection between the harmony and the melody.

Example 1 starts the solo with a bluesy phrase and some chord accents, before playing a line over the Eb7 to Bb7 change that includes some chord tone targeting. First, play through these shapes. The Edim7 is a passing chord. In a jazz blues, it's common to play the IV chord (Eb7, in this case) followed by a diminished 7 chord a half step up.

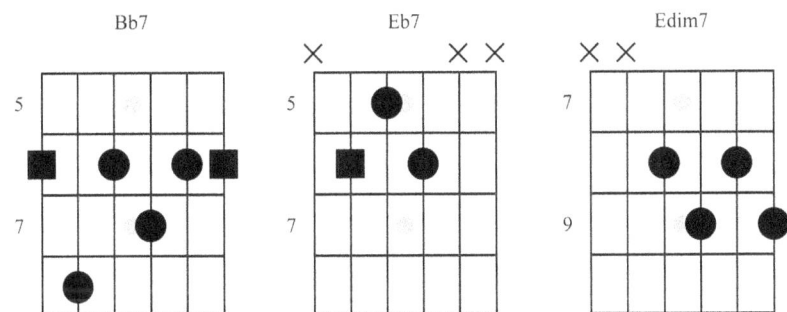

The line in bars 2-4 uses chromatic notes to approach chord tones of Bb7 from below and above. After playing a bluesy phrase over the Eb7, we land on a Bb note on the first beat of bar three. From there, we play a chromatic descent from Ab to F (the 5th of Bb7).

Next comes an "enclosure". This is where we have a target note in mind (the D that falls on beat 1 of bar four – the 3rd of Bb7) and enclose it by playing notes above and below it. A common enclosure pattern is to play a note above the target (Eb on the third string, 8th fret) then walk up to it chromatically from below (the C to Db to D movement).

Example 1a

Having a strong "map" of the chord shapes we're improvising over helps us to play lines that are much more melodic than scale patterns. In this next example, we move from chord IV of the blues to an Edim7 passing chord, back to the I chord. Next comes a common addition to the jazz blues in bar four where we play a G7.

There is a chain of logic that leads to playing this G7 chord.

We know that a standard blues progression has just three chords. In the key of Bb they are Bb7 (I), Eb7 (IV) and F7 (V).

A common move in jazz is to anticipate the V chord by placing its ii chord in front of it. I.e., Cm7 to F7. But we can take a further step backwards and anticipate that ii chord with *its* V chord. I.e., G7 to Cm7.

The end result is a harmonic sequence where G7 wants to resolve to Cm7, which sets up the movement to F7, which in turn wants to resolve to the I chord, Bb7.

In Example 1b, I added some extra colour to the G7 by implying a G7b9 sound. Thinking of this chord as a dominant 7b9 allows us to play a diminished arpeggio over it, and it's common to launch the arpeggio from the 3rd of the dominant chord (the B note on the 9th fret of the fourth string in this case).

Example 1b

The next example shows a simple way to move smoothly between the V (F7) and I (Bb7) chords. Start by visualising the Cm7 shape below, moving to the F7. The Bb7 shape used here is the standard barre chord shown in Example 1a.

In bar two, play an ascending F7 arpeggio (F, A, C, Eb) from the 3rd of the chord (A) and slide into the F note on the second string from a half step above. We are targeting the 3rd (D) of the Bb7 chord again by playing a note a half step above, then climbing chromatically from a whole step below.

Example 1c

In bar one of this example, think of the Bb7 shape below as supplying the beginning of the phrase, before we slip into a bluesy Bb Minor Pentatonic phrase. From there, a half step movement targets the 3rd of the Eb7 chord (based on the shape used in Example 1a).

In bar three, we need to visualise a new shape for Bb7. The Bb9 shape shown below (often played without the root note, indicated by a hollow circle) is a good guide to understand the melodic line. Notice that we use another "above and below" enclosure here.

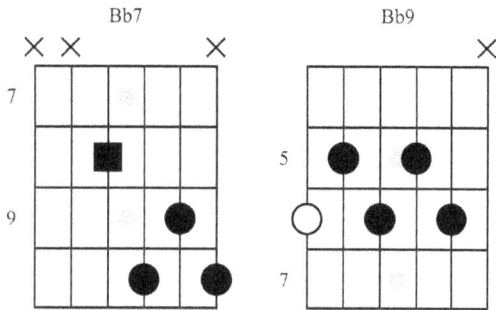

Example 1d

In this example, after an Eb7 chord accent, we spell out the passing Edim7 chord by playing its b5 (Bb) and bb7 (Db) notes, based around the inversion shape below.

For the Bb7 to G7 movement, visualise the shapes below. Over G7 we're thinking G7b9 again, which can be played using this 10th fret shape with its root note on the fifth string.

The Bb7 and G7b9 shapes move into a standard Cm7 barre chord in 8th position, then into the F7 shape below. While holding down the chords, look at where the melody notes fall around them and you'll see that they all sit close to the chord shapes.

This is a complex line with chromatic passing notes and enclosures, played at a brisk tempo. My advice is always to play through it very slowly at first, finding the most comfortable fingering and locking that into muscle memory.

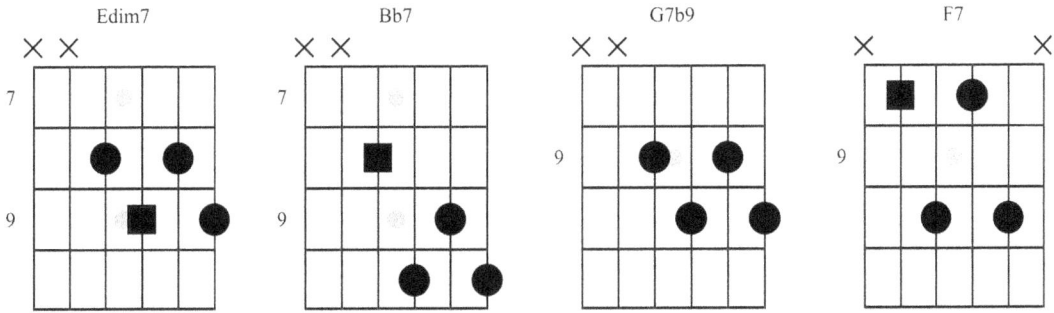

Example 1e

For this descending lick in the higher register we'll need to visualise new shapes for Bb7 and Eb7.

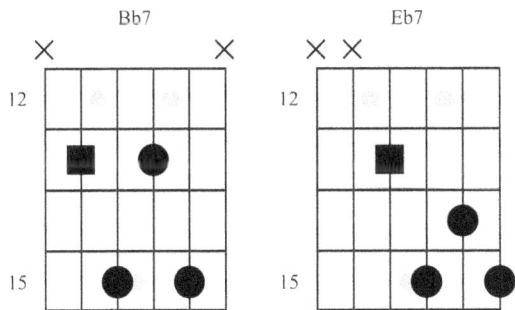

The line starts with a motif that repeats over the chord I to IV to I change. To play the descending lick in bars 3-4, start with your first finger on the first string 12th fret, and play the second string 15th fret with your third finger. When you get to the 12th fret of the second string, you'll play that note with your first finger then slide it down to the 11th fret.

When you get to the notes on the fourth string, play the fret 12 to 11 pull-off with your second and first fingers. Now bring over your pinkie to play the 14th fret of the fifth string, and use your third finger for the 13th fret. You can slide from the 11th fret to the 10th with your first finger, or play this as a pull-off.

Example 1f

This line begins with a chromatic descent to land on the 3rd (G) of Eb7. For the Bb7 to G7 change, I had in mind the chord shapes below. Using these voicings we can visualise both chords played in 8th position. Play the shapes and look at how the line fits around them.

Example 1g

We've now covered all the dominant 7th shapes you'll need, so that you can identify which is being used for a particular line. Analyse the following example and work out which chord voicings are being used in each position.

One hint: when it comes to bar four, for this lick I'm still visualising a 6th fret, sixth-string root Bb7 chord, treating the ii – V – I sequence in the way a blues player might approach it.

Work through the line slowly to find a fingering that is smooth and comfortable for you. This example contains some classic bebop phrases – the kind you might hear in a Charlie Parker solo. Once again, it's all about visualising the most important chord tones (primarily the 3rd and 7th, as well as the root) and targeting them with approach notes.

Example 1h

In this example, the pickup bar reveals the voicing of Eb7 to visualise. In bar two, the line is based around a standard 6th fret Bb7 barre chord. This is another example of how we can generate bebop-style phrasing by visualising the chord shape and using chromatic approach notes to target the important chord tones. In bars 4-8, we take the simple approach of outlining the bass notes of the chord changes.

Example 1i

Here's a fun, ascending run that uses chromatic approach notes to target chord tones. The run is aiming for the two-note chord that falls on beat 1 of Example 1k.

Example 1j

In the first part of this example, we use the guide tones of the chords to spell out the harmony. Guide tones are the 3rd and 7th intervals of any chord and, combined, they are the most important notes in defining the quality of the chord i.e., whether it's a dominant 7, a minor 7, etc. They are very useful for outlining the harmony of any chord progression with simple two-note shapes.

Example 1k

Play through the next example and work out which chord voicings you think were used to visualise and build the line. Hint: they're all standard 6th or 5th string root shapes we've used before, just in the higher register.

Example 1l

Do the same with this line and see if you've guessed correctly. Answers below! (Hint: I'm just visualising an F7 chord for both bars one and two.

Example 1m

Answer:

To end the solo with a contrast to the single-note lines, here is a typical Gypsy Jazz approach to playing through the changes with a chord solo. We could dedicate an entire book on its own to this topic, but I'll highlight three important features of this approach.

First, you're notice that all the chords are four-note forms using compact shapes, so that there is no need for any awkward stretches. This enables us to quickly move between shapes.

Second, they are all located on the top four strings or the middle four strings, which helps them to punch out and be heard when playing with a band.

Third, you could play only the highest note of each chord and you'd be left with a melodic line that makes sense in itself

This is the crux of the idea: we're playing a melodic line, but harmonising it into chords. When you experiment with chord soloing on your own, always remember you're playing a melody – but with chords!

Listen to all the famous Gypsy Jazz players and also Wes Montgomery to hear how effective chord soloing can be and how different players approach it.

Example 1n

Now that you've played every part of the solo, work through the entire piece. Over time, see how much of it you can memorise, but the main thing is to grab and absorb the licks that you like.

Example 1o – Full Solo

Cm7 F7 B♭7 G7 Cm7 F7
B♭7 E♭7 B♭7
E♭7 Edim7 B♭7 G7
Cm7 F7 B♭7 G7 Cm7 F7
B♭7 E♭7 B♭7

E♭7 Edim7 B♭7 G7
Cm7 F7 B♭7 G7 Cm7 F7
B♭7 E♭7 B♭7
E♭7 Edim7 B♭7 G7
Cm7 F7 B♭7 G7 Cm7 F7

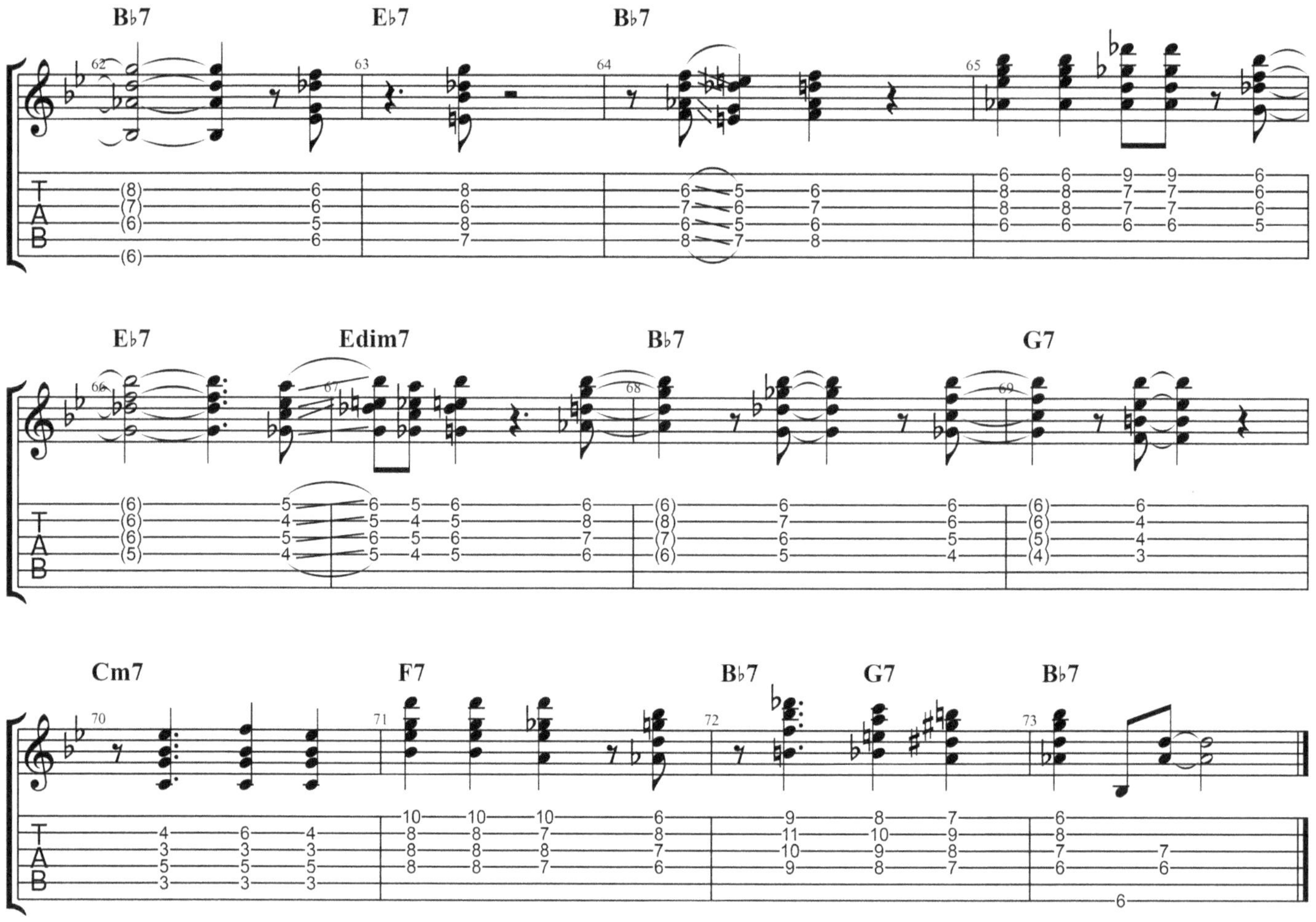
B♭7
E♭7
B♭7
E♭7
Edim7
B♭7
G7
Cm7
F7
B♭7
G7
B♭7

Chapter Two – Bossa Dorado

Bossa Dorado was composed by Dorado Schmitt, a French Gypsy Jazz guitarist and violinist. The tune has since become a must-know standard in the Gypsy Jazz repertoire. Schmitt grew up in a musical family and was heavily influenced by Django Reinhardt. He later played in a Gypsy Jazz ensemble that included Django's son, Babik, and has also worked with guitar legends Biréli Lagrène and Angelo Debarre.

Unlike a Latin Jazz bossa nova, a Gypsy Jazz bossa is usually played with a driving rhythm guitar style that outlines straight 1/8th notes. This style of Gypsy Jazz bossa has a real forward momentum to it and is typically played a little more up-tempo than you might expect from a bossa nova.

We can think of the line in bars 1-2 as moving between three adjacent voicings of Dm7. Although we're only picking out a couple of notes from each shape, it's useful to be able to visualise these shapes and understand how they connect across the fretboard. In bar three, think of a standard E7 barre chord at the 12th fret.

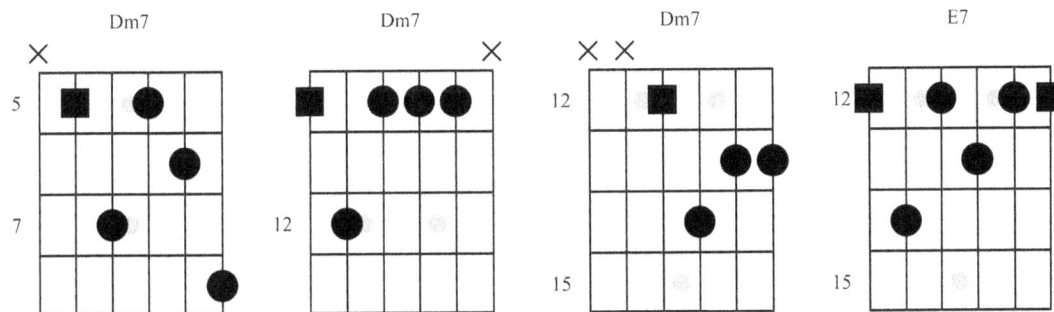

Example 2a

For the next part of the tune we're thinking around these shapes:

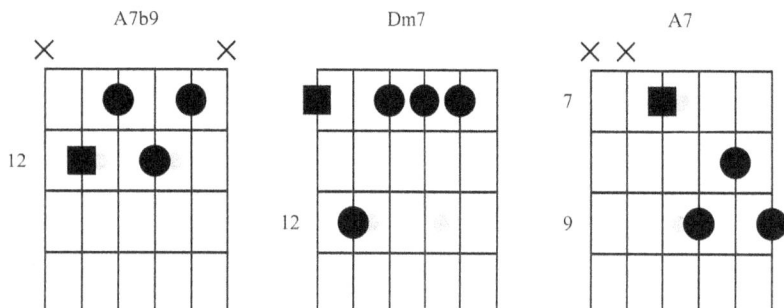

We start this line by playing an outside tension note which resolves to a chord tone of A7b9 (G, the b7). Playing a chromatic note that resolves to a chord tone which falls on the beat, is a very effective way of creating tension and release, shown here in its simplest form.

Bar two is a good example of how we can weave around a chord shape (the 10th position Dm7 shown above) and create an interesting phrase using articulation. The note on the 11th fret of the second string is outside of the shape and is the b13 (or #5) of the chord, but is played fleetingly to add a nice tension.

Over the A7 chord, we're playing a kind of enclosure idea. The focal point is the E note at the 9th fret, the 5th of A7. Around it we play notes below and above, but we keep referencing that E.

Example 2b

In this line, I'm visualising a 5th position Dm7 chord moving up to the 10th position shape. In bar five, we can play a rootless voicing of A7b9 in the same zone of the neck by relocating one finger onto the top string from the shape we saw in Example 2b.

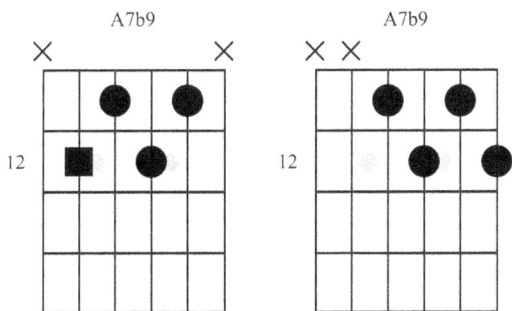

Notice the enclosure that emphasises the root note of the Dm chord, which begins halfway through bar six, so that we land on the D note on beat 1 of bar seven.

Example 2c

For the D7 and E7 chords here, we can think of the same sixth string root shape we used back in Example 2a. Notice that all the chords in this example are located in the same zone of the neck. This helps us to create a motif-driven line, making small variations to accommodate each chord change.

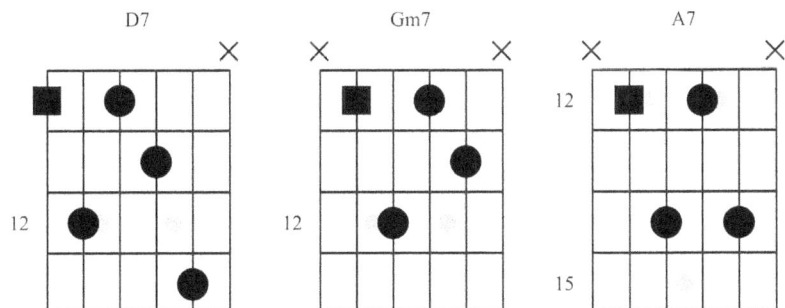

The motif idea, stated in bar one, is to play a D7b9 arpeggio from F# (3rd). We repeat the motif, then play an enclosure that targets the Bb (3rd) of the Gm7 chord.

Then we start a new motif around a pedal tone – the D note on the fourth string, 12th fret. D is a note common to both Gm7 and E7 chords, so we only need to reference one note (G#) in bar five to highlight that we've changed from Gm7 to E7.

Example 2d

Using two chord shapes we've already seen, this line moves from 5th to 10th position for the Dm chord. Then we can choose notes around the E7 shape below for bar three.

After ascending a Dm9 arpeggio in bar one, we play another simple motif idea on one string that is adapted for the E7 chord and lands on the 3rd in bar four.

Example 2e

This line is based around this useful A7b9 shape at the 5th fret. I usually play this voicing with my thumb over the neck for the bottom string, then my first and second fingers for the fourth and second strings. My third and fourth fingers fret the third and first strings.

Notice how the descending chromatics on the second, fourth and fifth strings are connecting our chord tones. On the second string we're descending chromatically from the b7 of the chord to the 5th (G to E). On the fourth string we're connecting the b9 to the b7 (Bb to G), and on the fifth string we're connecting the 5th to the 3rd (E to C#). From there, we move into a standard 5th position Dm7 voicing.

At circa 160bpm, this 1/16th note run is challenging. Follow our usual advice: map out the line slowly to achieve a comfortable fingering approach, and to get the sound of it in your head. Then practice it in isolation, gradually bringing it up to tempo.

There are a couple of ways to finger this lick. For the ascending part at the start of the line I use all four fingers, with one finger per fret starting with my first finger on the 5th fret. However, for the descending part, I use only my first three fingers for all of the notes, shifting position as the strings change. This is what feels comfortable for me, but feel free to experiment to see what works best for you.

In terms of picking, the descending part of this lick has either two or four notes per string, so we can use alternate (down up, down up) picking starting on the Bb note on the 6th fret, first string. However, for the ascending part before that, where there are three notes on adjacent strings, I would opt to economy pick. I.e., I'll push through the strings with downstrokes.

If you like to think scalically as well as around chord shapes, this line could also be viewed as coming from the D Harmonic Minor scale with some added chromatic passing tones.

Example 2f

The lick in bar one connects two standard A7 voicings. Even though the chord chart says A7b9, we can reduce that to plain A7 chord voicings, then focus on locating where the colour tones sit around the shapes. In bar two, the line is built around an inversion of Dm7 with the root note located on the second string.

For the E7 line in bar three, we're working around a standard E7 barre chord at the 12th fret. The notes of the lick stick very closely to the shape in this instance, and one chromatic note is introduced on the fourth string to keep the line moving until the lick ends on the 3rd of the chord.

Example 2g

For the next passage of A7b9, here is another fast line made up mostly of 1/8th note triplets. I'm sure you'll hear right away that it uses the "dominant-diminished connection" that we've previously discussed, as we play a diminished arpeggio from the 3rd (C#) of A7. We are visualising the 12th fret, fifth string root A7b9 shape seen in Example 2b. Work out which Dm7 voicing would make the most sense to create the line in bar three.

Playing continuous 1/8th triplets is hard to do consistently, so work at this line until you can play it smoothly.

Example 2h

This line begins by moving from a 10th position Dm7 down to the 5th position shape. In bar three, the E7 chord I'm visualising is played as part of the melodic idea. You can think of standard 5th position shapes for both A7 and Dm7 chords in bars 5-8.

Notice how chromatic approach notes are used in the phrasing here to lead into strong chord tones. Approach notes are very useful when we want to play passages of continuous 1/8th notes, and help to keep up the line's interest and momentum.

Example 2i

Bar one of this example hints at the chord voicing I visualised for D7 – a fragment of a D7b9 chord without the D root note. The line in bar two is a diminished arpeggio played over the implied D7b9, but the first part of the phrase (we'd normally launch from F#, the 3rd of D7) is left out, and instead we begin from a C note – the b7 of the chord. In bar three, we spell out the Gm chord voicing with single notes around the shape below.

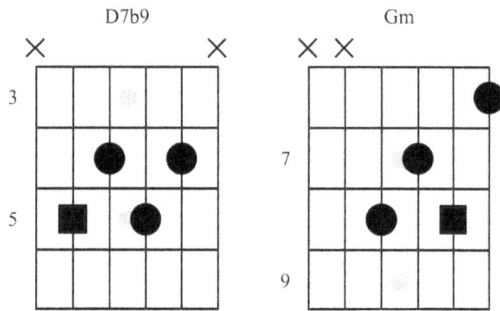

Example 2j

Here's another example of how to incorporate a diminished arpeggio launching from the 3rd of the dominant chord. The phrase that begins at the end of bar two, and includes the first three notes of bar three, targets the A root note of the chord. Then we play the diminished arpeggio from the C# note on the fourth string, 11th fret.

This line is another test of your ability to play even 1/8th note triplets over the boss nova pulse. Aim for consistent volume as well as timing.

Example 2k

You can think of this final line as being structured around a 10th position Dm7 barre chord, moving to a 7th position E7. For the A7b9 chord, we're thinking around the 12th fret shape again.

The line in bars 5-6 is a challenging one, consisting of straight 1/16th notes. For the fingering, begin by fretting the fifth string at the 12th fret with your second finger. Play the notes on the fourth string with the first and third fingers. Next, play the 12th and 14th frets of the third string with your first and third fingers. You'll play the C# note on fret 14 of the second string with your second finger, and from there the rest of the fingering is intuitive.

For the descending chromatic notes on strings 2, 3 and 4, I prefer to use just three fingers. I start each string with my third finger, descend three notes (one with each finger), and finally play the last note by shifting the first finger down a fret.

Example 21

You've worked through every part of the solo. Now have a listen to the audio of the whole thing and work towards playing along with it. Whenever you encounter a difficult passage or a part that is consistently tripping you up, work on it in isolation and eventually it will click.

Example 2m – Full Solo

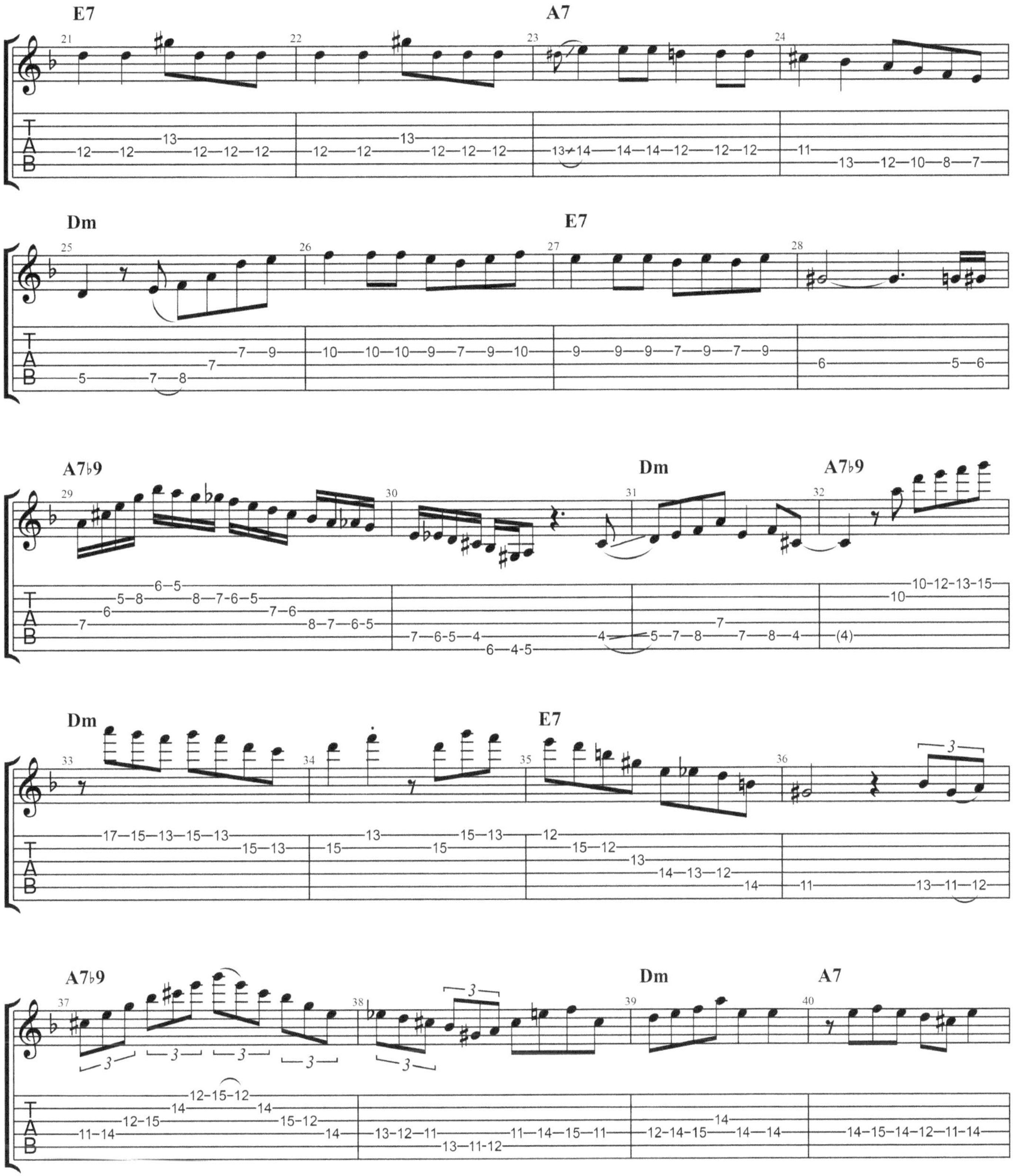
E7
A7
Dm
E7
A7♭9
Dm
A7♭9
Dm
E7
A7♭9
Dm
A7
T
A
B

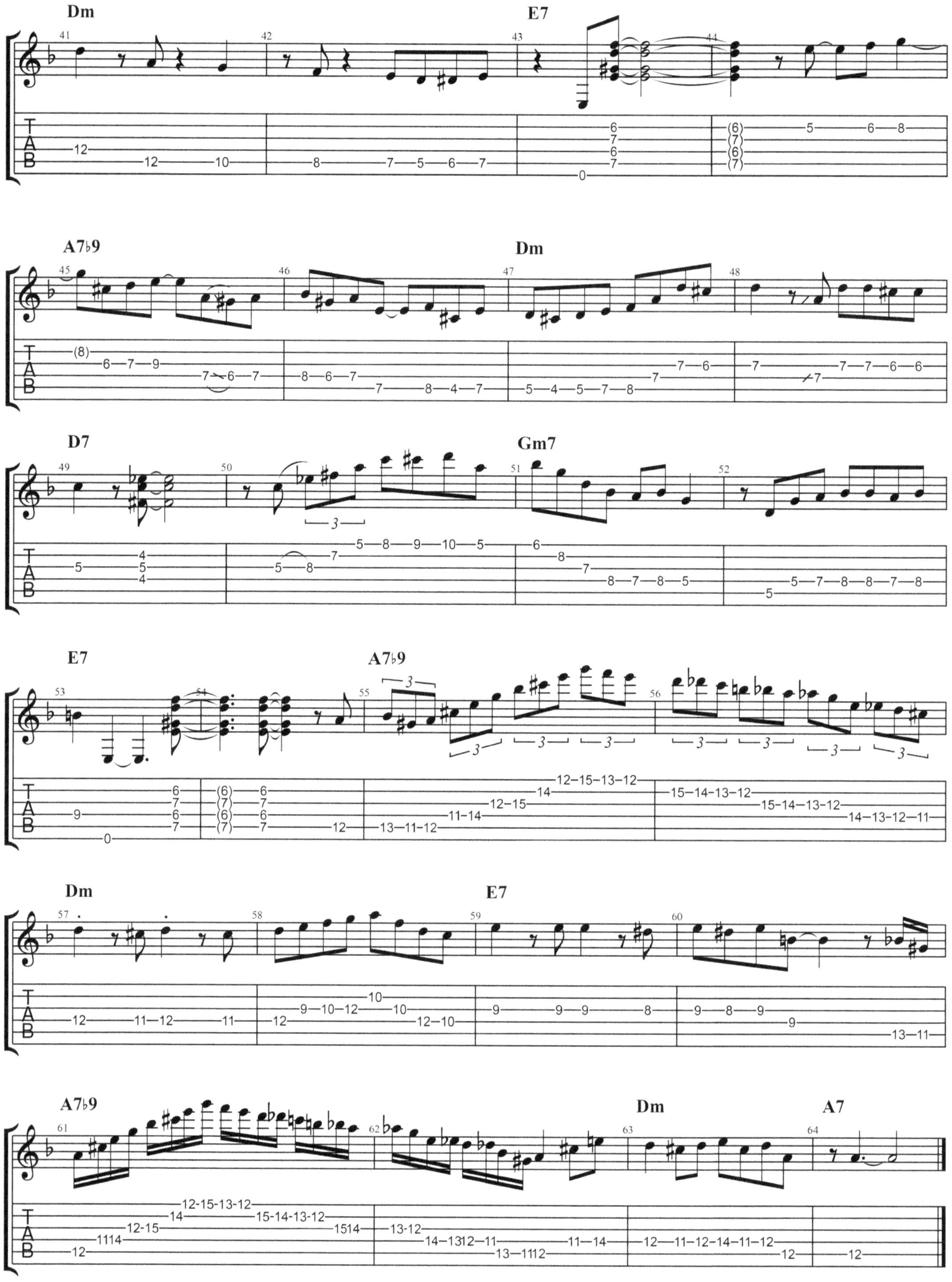
Dm
E7
A7♭9
Dm
D7
Gm7
E7
A7♭9
Dm
E7
A7♭9
Dm
A7

Chapter Three – 12-Bar Blues in G Minor Pt 1

The minor 12-bar sequence is one of the most commonly played chord sequences in Gypsy Jazz. Django wrote two very popular tunes based on this sequence – *Blues en Mineur* and *Swing 48*. Both of these tunes are played extensively at gigs and jam sessions and offer a great vehicle for improvisation.

There are a number of recordings of *Blues en Mineur* and I'm sure Django must have really enjoyed jamming on the chord sequence as there is even a version of him playing violin on it. Recorded in Brussels in 1942 as a duet with pianist Ivor de Bie, Django starts on violin and during the piano solo swaps to guitar!

The minor blues chord sequence is so prolific in Gypsy Jazz that we're going to dedicate two whole chapters to it. It is nearly always played in G Minor, which is a great key for the guitar as it gives us the whole range of the fingerboard from the low root on the sixth string 3rd fret, to the high G on the top string, 15th fret. You'll learn two etudes in this chapter and the next, which will help you to see how to build variations on a theme.

Here is a short introduction to start off the tune. It sets us up to resolve to Gm by playing the V chord (D7).

Example 3a

This tune has a simple harmony and contains just four chords, so our focus will be on discovering different voicings for those chords. The opening line of the etude can be thought of as moving between these two Gm voicings.

At the end of the lick, a passing Db note makes a dissonant b5 sound over the Gm. This adds both an element of surprise, by introducing a little tension, and leads chromatically into the Eb note in bar one of Example 3c (a chord tone of Cm).

Example 3b

You'll be familiar with standard Cm7 chord shapes at the 3rd and 8th frets, but the frets 5-7 zone of the fretboard can often be overlooked or ignored. Yet, there are several nice Cm shapes to be found there, including this simple Cm triad inversion with the 3rd in the bass. Play the chord, then look at the melodic line to see how it fits around it.

Example 3c

Think of this shape for the Eb7 chord in the next example, then slide it down a half step to provide the focal point for the D7, moving into a regular Gm7 barre chord at the 3rd fret.

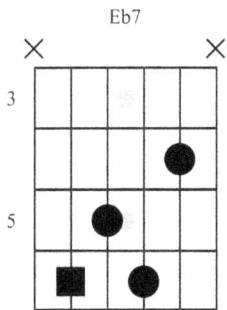

By now you should be quite the expert at recognising a diminished lick when you hear one. In bar two, we treat the D7 chord as though it's a D7b9 and launch the diminished arpeggio from its 3rd (F#). This takes us up to an A note on the top string. From here we can play a half step movement to the 6th fret to play a chord tone of Gm.

Example 3d

The next section is all based around 3rd position barre chords of Gm7 and Cm7. When creating improvised melodies, beyond note choice, two of our most useful tools are *rhythm* and *space*.

In the pickup bar, the first note is played on beat 2&. With strong rhythmic phrasing we can form a motif using just three notes. A great practice exercise is to record a one-chord vamp, then improvise over it limiting yourself to just a few notes. With limited note choice, you'll be forced to become inventive with your rhythmic phrasing. As easy way to get into this is to play the same phrase but move it to different beats (or beat subdivisions) of the bar.

In bar two we rest for a 1/4 note before finishing the phrase, then leave more space before playing a variation on the motif in bars 2-3. Although the motif gets adapted as we go through the bars, you can hear that the melodic theme continues throughout.

Example 3e

This line begins with the Eb7 shape below in mind. In bar two, the presence of an Eb note, which falls on beat 3, hints that the chord we're visualising next is D7b9, rather than simply moving the Eb7 shape down a half step. In bar three, we can think of the Gm triad inversion below as our point of reference.

The short run up in the pickup bar is targeting a Db note (b7 of Eb7) on beat 1 of bar one. The phrase that spans the end of bar one into bar two targets the F# chord tone of D7 that falls on beat 2, and we also drop the D root note on beat 4. The strategy of playing chord tones on the down-beats continues for the Gm chord, where we play the 9th on beat 1, the root on beat 2, the b3 on beat 3 and the b7 on beat 4.

Example 3f

For this next example, think around this 10th fret voicing for the Gm bars. For bars 5-6 we move between the two Cm7 shapes below.

Repetition is an important part of blues language and can be very effective when used over a static chord. Bars 1-3 use a simple two-note motif, played with a half step slide into the first note. The notes are the 5th and b7 of the Gm chord. After stating the motif in bar one, it gets turned into a repeating lick in bars 2-3.

In bar four, a short phrase ends with a tension note that resolves to the 5th of the Cm chord. Bars 4-7 weave around the chord shapes a lot, so be sure to check out the phrasing on the audio example to hear how it should sound.

Example 3g

Here's a fun line that has a theme: play a phrase followed by a single lower note that falls on the first beat of the bar.

Think in terms of a standard Eb7 barre chord at the 11th fret, moving to a D7 barre at the 10th, then a fifth-string root Gm at the 10th.

For each chord, we're dropping in a lower 7th interval. Over the Eb7 chord it's the b7 (Db). For the D7 chord it's a C, also the b7. But for the Gm we're playing a major 7 rather than the b7. This Gb/F# note implies that the underlying chord is a GmMaj7.

Example 3h

This line uses the voicings we looked at in Example 3g. The Gm7 shape at the 10th fret really lends itself to this repeating motif.

Part of the motif is the descending four-note phrase that begins on the second string, 13th fret. Notice how we get more out of this phrase by placing it on different beats of the bar. In bar one it begins on beat 3. In bar two we play a longer 1/4 note, so that the phrase begins on beat 2. Then, in bar three we begin the phrase right on beat 1. Rhythmic displacement is a tool you should always consider using when improvising.

The 1/8th note triplet phrase that begins on beat 4 of bar three is challenging to play cleanly at 200bpm. I suggest working on just the cluster of notes organised into triplets to begin with, after listening carefully to the audio, then add the other notes around that phrase.

Example 3i

This line uses standard voicings for all three chords, which you should be able to identify with no trouble.

In this example we're using the idea of weaving around the chord shape then picking a chord tone to play that will lead smoothly to a chord tone of the next chord via a half step movement.

This takes a bit of thought and forward planning but is a great skill to develop, as it really grounds the harmony. At the end of bar one, we play a G note. This is the 3rd of Eb7 and a half step above F#, which is the 3rd of D7. Because we're moving in half steps, this sounds like a tension and resolution.

We do the same thing at the end of bar two to set up the Gm chord. This time we're moving from F# (3rd of D7) to G, the root of Gm – another half step resolution.

When you have some spare time to practice, try working through some chord changes. Visualise the chord shapes and work out ways of moving from one to the next using half step note movements wherever possible.

Example 3j

We finish this etude with a chord solo. It's useful to study a passage like this when thinking about your chord playing, because it helps to open your eyes to new ideas, and you might discover combinations of voicings you hadn't thought of putting together.

Example 3k

When you're feeling confident, have a go at the full solo. Also have some fun just jamming over the backing track, trying out your favourite licks.

Example 3l – Full Solo

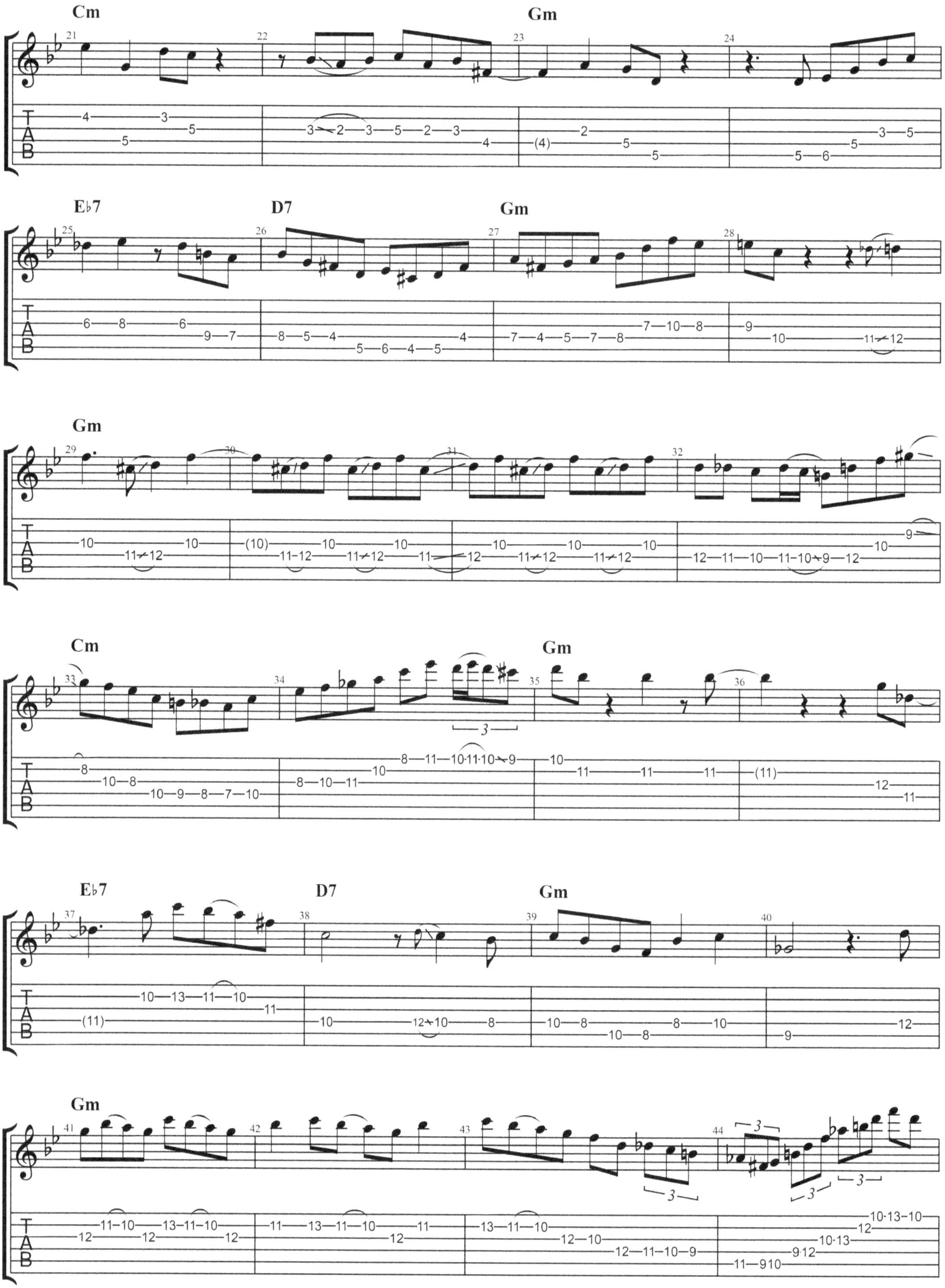
Cm
Gm
E♭7
D7
Gm
Gm
Cm
Gm
E♭7
D7
Gm
Gm

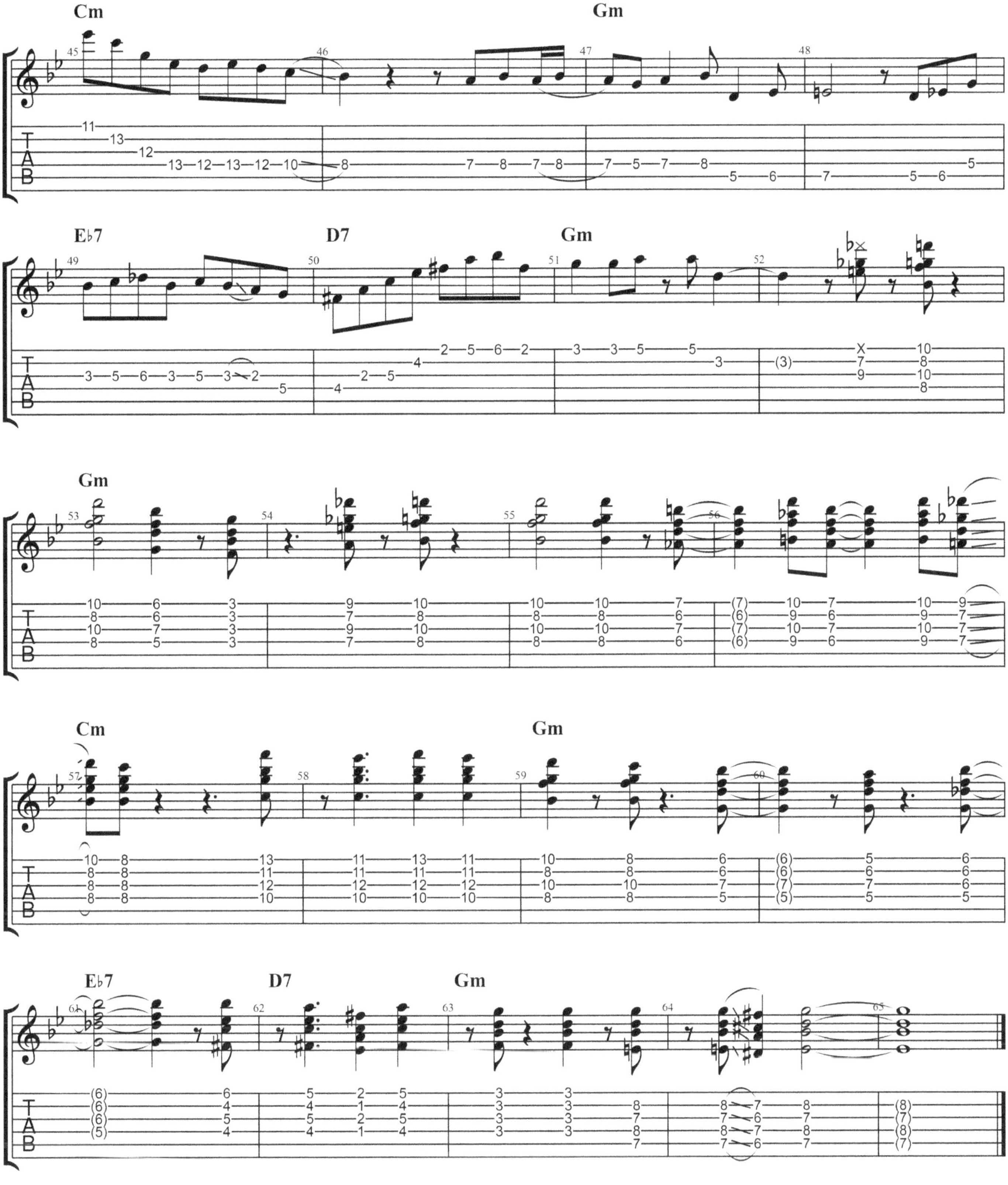
Cm
Gm
E♭7
D7
Gm
Gm
Cm
Gm
E♭7
D7
Gm

Chapter Four – 12-Bar Blues in G Minor Pt2

As mentioned in the previous chapter, the minor blues form is so important in Gypsy Jazz that it's worth spending some more time exploring it. We previously looked at all the chord shapes necessary for you to understand where the melodic lines come from, so in this chapter we'll turn our attention to the phrasing.

Example 4a is the introduction that sets up the tune. It's similar to how we started in Chapter Three, but with a little variation in bars 3-4.

Example 4a

We ease into the solo with a simple motif that has repeating notes on the fourth string, moving from Bb to A to G. A really useful device in jazz soloing is to find note selections that work over several chords in the progression. Over Gm, these notes represent the b3, 9th and root respectively.

In bar five, we omit the Bb in order to alter the phrasing over Cm, and just play the A to G movement. The Bb note would have worked, as it's the b7 of Cm, but A is the richer sounding 13th and G is the 5th.

We use the notes again for the Eb7 chord in bar nine. This time Bb is the 5th of the chord and G is the 3rd. Here I opted to omit the A note. It's the #11 interval and would imply an altered dominant chord. This would have added a little more tension than I thought was needed at this point within the solo.

The D7 chord in bar ten is where we have to modify the motif further – the F# and A notes being the 3rd and 5th of the D7. These two notes also surround the target note of G, which is the root of our next chord, Gm.

Example 4b

This line over Gm moves through three voicings of the chord, ascending the neck. Can you work out what they are? If you're struggling to see it, I recommend using an online fretboard mapping tool. Type in the notes of a Gm7 chord to see the notes distributed across the neck, and work out which chords shapes would be most helpful in visualising the line.

For those who like to relate ideas to scales as well as chord shapes, this lick comes from the G Harmonic Minor scale, with the exception of the C# note at the end of bar two. This note is a b5 tension I dropped in to spice up the idea and is played with "delayed resolution". I.e., it doesn't quickly resolve but lingers for a beat.

Example 4c

You should have no difficulty in identifying the chord shapes to visualise in this example. It's worth pointing out what is happening in bar two of this line, as it's a useful technique to add to your arsenal of ideas.

Jazz musicians often *imply* chord changes that are not written on the chord chart. The purpose of doing so is to create the opportunity for more movement, which allows us to add different colours to our melodic lines.

It's very common, for example, for dominant 7 chords to be preceded with their ii chord. E.g., if F7 is written on the chart, we might play a melodic idea that moves from Cm7 (ii) into F7 (V).

But we can also flip that idea around and play an F7 idea over Cm. Play an F7 chord, then play and listen to the line in bar two. You'll hear that the idea is very close to a diminished arpeggio played from the 3rd of F7 (which an additional note thrown in).

Without thinking about and visualising this implied chord change, we probably wouldn't have come up with the idea of playing an Adim7 arpeggio over Cm!

Example 4d

To end this chorus of the blues we spell out the Eb7 and D7 chords, choosing notes around 11th and 10th fret barre chords.

At the end of bar three, this short three-note lick is a staple idea in Gypsy Jazz. When playing minor chords, Gypsy Jazz guitarists will often voice them as minor 6 chords rather than minor 7s – and this is one of the characteristics often associated with the Gypsy Jazz sound. These three notes move from the 5th (D) of Gm, to the #5 (Eb) to the 6th (E) to create that mood.

Example 4e

This line continues the minor 6 mood in bars 1-3 by punctuating the lick with a lower E note (6th) on the fourth string. We copy the phrasing of the G minor motif in bar five over Cm, but here the note are the root and b3 of the chord. Add some bluesy articulation in bars 7-8.

Example 4f

Over the turnaround section, this time we're playing a line constructed mostly from 1/8th notes. A good workout for the practice room is to take a jazz standard and try to play continuous 1/8th notes over the chord changes. The result should sound something like a classical etude as the notes weave around the harmony.

This is more difficult to do than it sounds and is a great way of challenging our ability to improvise smoothly over chord changes. It not only tests our knowledge of where the important chord tones sit, it forces us to get creative with our phrasing and to use passing notes to fill any gaps.

It can sound boring if we play continuous 1/8th notes when soloing, but longer 1/8th note passages can be very effective when used sparingly.

Example 4g

Being able to comp for yourself is a good skill to develop. It can be particularly useful when you're playing with just a bass player as a duo, or playing as a trio with bass and drums, so that you can remind your audience of the harmony you're playing over. But it's also useful to help develop your phrasing and make it more concise. One of the ways I like to approach this is by imagining the horn section of a big band playing in between my phrases. This is demonstrated in Example 4h.

Take this idea into your next practice session. Play to a metronome or drum groove without any chordal accompaniment. This will help encourage you to keep suggesting the harmony you're improvising over with chords. Aim for short musical phrases that you could sing in one breath, then accompany them with the big band horn section chord stabs.

Example 4h

Here's a variation on this idea. This time, instead of "interrupting" our line with a mid-bar chord accent, we wait until bar four. We're also taking the opportunity to hint at an impending chord change, playing a partial Eb7 chord ahead of the beat.

Example 4i

As we've discussed previously, it's also good to be able to solo with chords, and the final two excerpts from the solo do this. Remember, we're not aimlessly stringing together any voicings we can think of for each chord – the key here is to invent a melody, usually on the first string, then find appropriate voicings to support it. This can be tricky and challenging to work out, but the end result is always very rewarding. Play through both examples slowly and try to commit the chord voicings to memory.

Example 4j

Example 4k

Now it's time to put all the ideas together and play through the full solo.

Example 4l – Full Solo

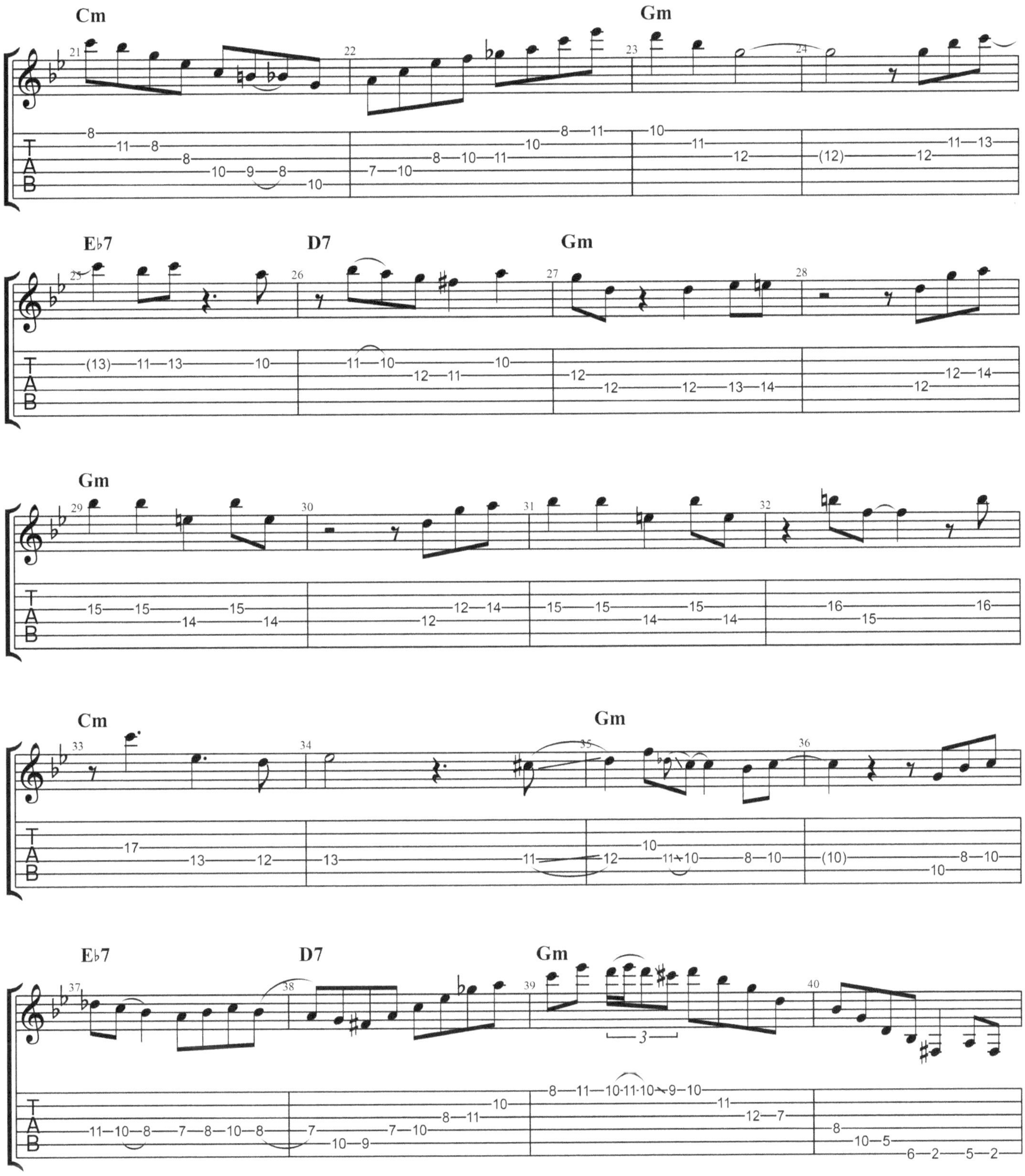
Cm
Gm
E♭7
D7
Gm
Gm
Cm
Gm
E♭7
D7
Gm
TAB

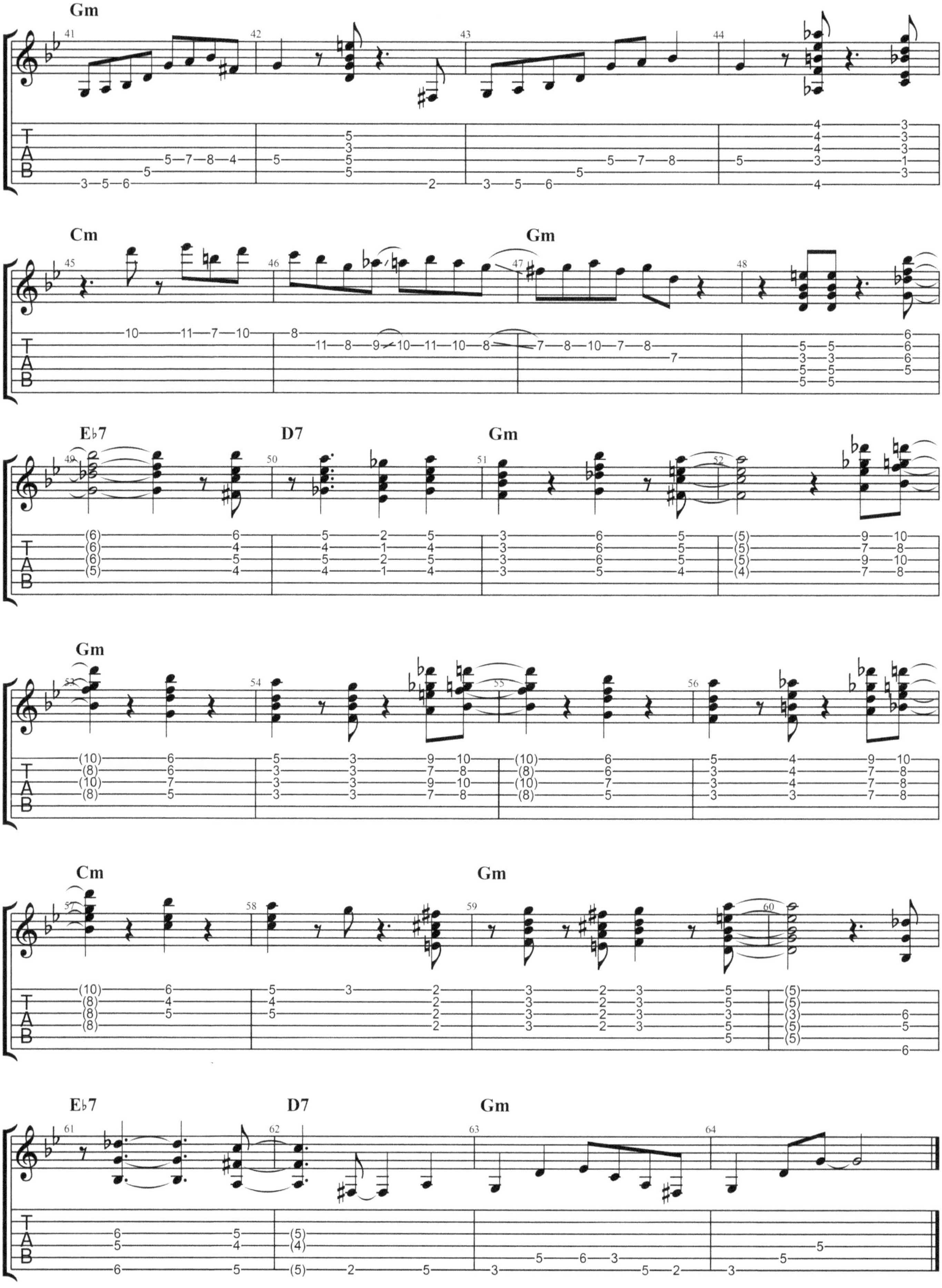
Gm
Cm
Gm
E♭7
D7
Gm
Gm
Cm
Gm
E♭7
D7
Gm
TAB

Chapter Five – Joseph Joseph

The song *Joseph Joseph* was adapted by Sammy Cahn and Saul Chaplin from an original Yiddish song (*Oh Yossel Yossel*, composed in 1923 by Samuel Steinberg and his wife, the celebrated Yiddish actress, Nellie Casman). The Cahn/Chaplin adaptation became a huge hit when it was recorded by The Andrews Sisters in 1938.

Although Django didn't actually record a version of this tune, it has become very popular amongst Gypsy Jazz players. As it features a very catchy melody, it's often played up tempo with lots of energy. It's a great tune to have some fun on.

For the opening of the solo, we position ourselves around the Am7 shape below. With its strong movement between Am and E7 chords, this song has a distinctive Gypsy Jazz Minor feel to it, and this is reflected in its melody. In Example 5a we play a line that hints at that melody while creating its own motif. Notice that the opening phrase repeats and we play just one note different at the end to highlight the coming E7 chord change (G#, the 3rd).

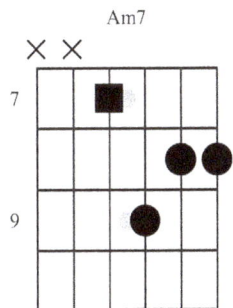

Example 5a

The lick in bar one here is based around the standard E7 shape below. We're played a diminished arpeggio over this chord, as we've done before, but this time launching straight from the root of the E7, rather than the 3rd (G#).

When the line descends, we're peppering that arpeggio with lots of chromatic passing notes to help create a flowing phrase that is typical of up tempo Gypsy Jazz improvisation. Aim for an even volume and good picking consistency as you play this long 1/8th note passage.

In bars 6-7, the second voicing of E7 below is the best reference point, and this shape leads nicely into a standard, 5th fret Am7 shape.

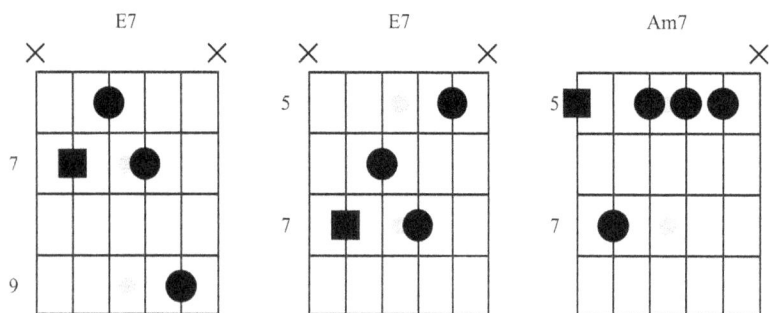

Example 5b

The next line is based around the shape below, but jumps out of it to play lower and higher A Minor scale notes on either side. The melody targets the 5th (E) of the Am chord on the first string, 12th fret, and also it's b3 (C) in different locations.

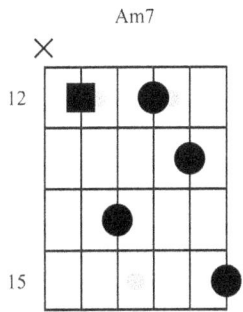

Am7

Example 5c

Based around the 12th fret, fifth string root A7b9 shape we used back in Chapter Two, here is another diminished idea. Rather than launching from the 3rd, we play a variation here before the ascending diminished arpeggio.

First, we descend chromatically to target the 3rd (C#) of the chord. Next, the three-note phrase in the middle of bar one is a chromatic enclosure. The target note is the A root, and we play a note a half step above it, then a half step below it, before playing the A.

After that phrase, we then launch the diminished lick from the 3rd.

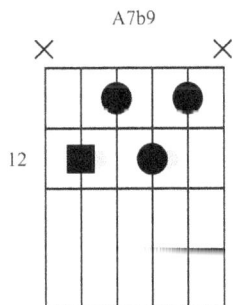

A7b9

Example 5d

This example opens with a rhythmic motif in bars 1-2 that is repeated in bars 3-4. A motif can be a note-for-note repetition of an idea, or it can use different notes but mimic the phrasing. Here, everything about the shape of the line and its rhythm is identical, but the notes have been changed to fit the Bb6 and Am chords. In bars 5-7 we can use just a few notes to navigate these three chords, with a half step bend helping to spell out the F7 chord.

Example 5e

The next example is long because we build from a simple, repetitive motif over the Am chord into a repeating hammer-on/pull-off phrase that continues for several bars over E7. This idea is based around standard shapes for Am and E7, with root notes on the fifth and sixth strings respectively.

I recommend slowing down the hammer-on/pull-off phrases to begin with and programming the movement into muscle memory. This way, when you speed things up, you'll have the correct technique needed to play the lick cleanly and evenly.

The articulated motif begins properly in bar five, but is preceded by two pick-up notes at the end of bar four. These two notes are actually part of the phrase and are used to launch the idea.

Over the Am in bars 5-6, play the lick like this:

- Hold down the 13th fret with the first finger and pick that note with a downstroke

- Hammer onto the 15th fret with the third finger

- Pull off from the 15th to the 13th with the third finger

- Shift the first finger down from the 13th to the 12th fret, picking the note on the 12th fret with a downstroke

- Play the 15th fret with the third finger again, picking the note with an upstroke

With the hammer-on/pull-off motion played as 1/8th note triplets, and the other two notes being straight 1/8ths, we create a five-note phrase and can fit two of them into a bar.

When we change to the E7 chord, the motif needs to be adapted. Because we don't need to stretch as far to play this melodic figure, we can use the first and second fingers. Apart from this, we execute the lick in exactly the same way.

Example 5f

To create some contrast, here's a chordal idea. When we play single-note melodic lines, we often use passing notes to target a specific note we're aiming for. We can do the same with chords, using them to "approach" target chords from above or below.

There is an implied chord change idea here. In bar four, our target chord is an Em7b5 at the 7th fret. We approach this from below by playing two chromatic passing chords. Although Em7b5 is not written on the chart, we're implying that bars 4-7 are a minor ii – V – I: Em7b5 – A7b9 – Dm.

Example 5g

We have already noted that the Gypsy Jazz sound often favours the use of 6th chords. This applies to major as well as minor chords, and the line at the beginning of this example is built around a common sixth string root voicing of Bb6.

From there, we move into a standard 5th fret Am, then to the simple dominant 7th shape below, starting with F7 and moving down a half step to E7 before returning to the Am chord. In this example you'll see again how we can take a simple motif phrase and adapt it to fit the next chord.

In bar five, notice the bend on beat 1. Although string bending isn't as prevalent in Gypsy Jazz as some other styles, Django often used half-step bends in his playing. Here I'm using a half-step bend up to the b7 of the F7 chord.

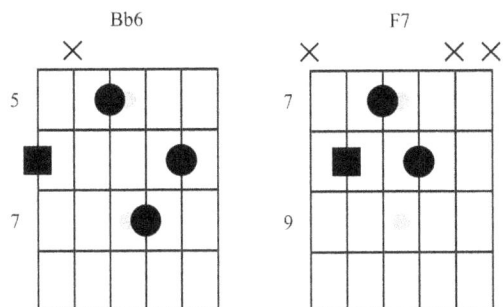

Example 5h

Now it's time to work on playing the full solo all the way through. Have fun jamming over the backing track too.

Example 5i – Full Solo

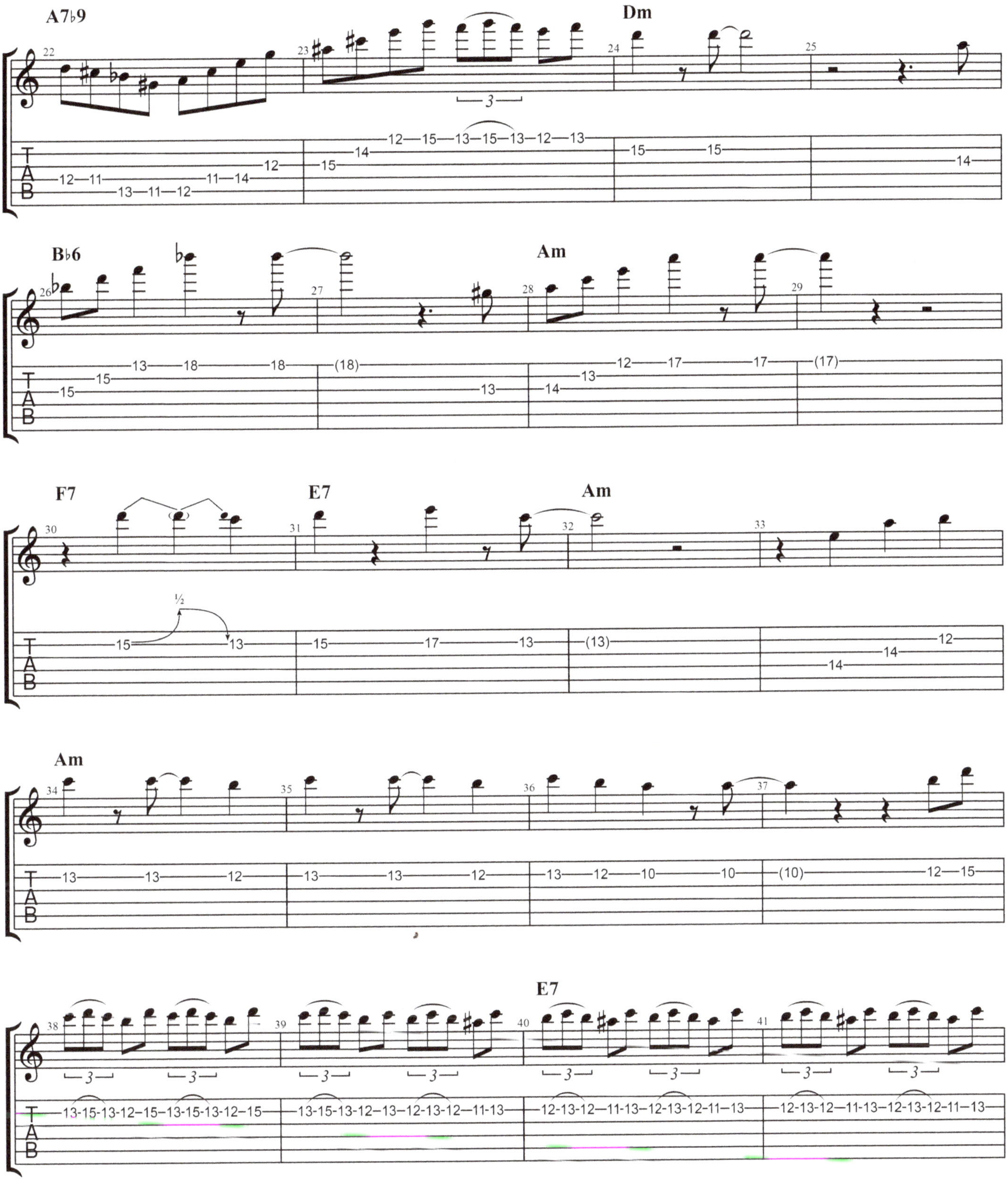
A7♭9
Dm
B♭6
Am
F7
E7
Am
Am
E7

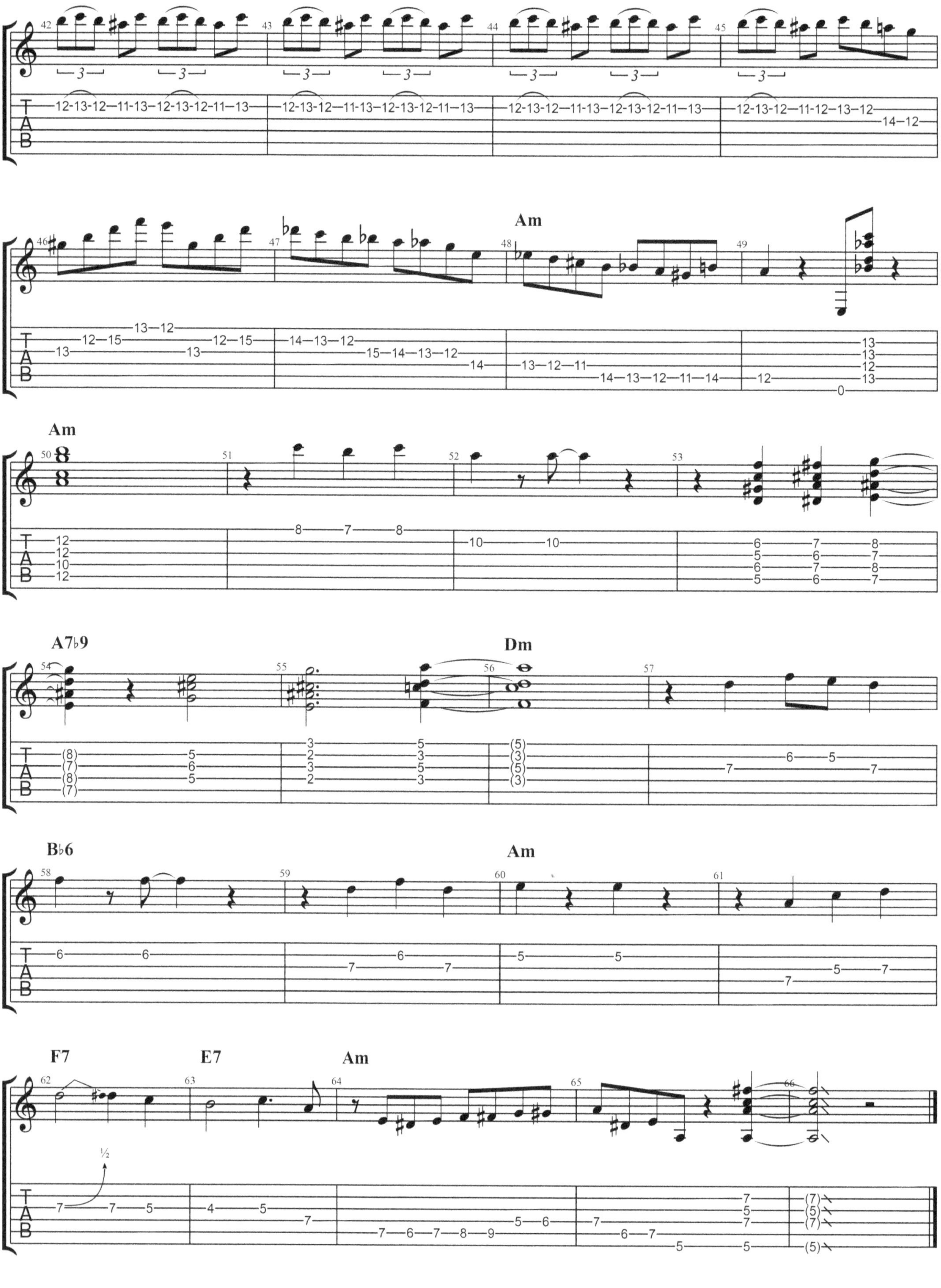
Am
Am
A7♭9
Dm
B♭6
Am
F7
E7
Am

Chapter Six – Lady Be Good

Oh, Lady Be Good! was written in 1924 by George and Ira Gershwin and was the title song of the Broadway musical *Lady, Be Good!* starring Fred and Adele Astaire. It was recorded in Paris in 1934 by Django Reinhardt and Stéphane Grappelli with the Quintette du Hot Club de France, and numerous cover versions by well-known artists have been released down the years.

Gershwin's original tempo instructions for the tune stated that it should be played, "slowly and gracefully," but jazz musicians have nearly always preferred to play it as a danceable, mid-tempo swinging tune, or an up-tempo vehicle for soloing. It lends itself well to either approach. In this chapter, we're playing it at 180bpm, but mostly with an 1/8th note swinging feel.

Here's a syncopated chord intro to start us off.

Example 6a

This tune has some lovely chord changes and throughout this etude we'll focus on articulating them as clearly as possible, using some bebop devices to spell out the harmony and move smoothly from chord to chord.

In the first four bars of this example, you should visualise the 8th fret C7 shape below, moving into a CAGED system "D" Shape voicing of G major. This leads nicely into a fifth string root voicing of E7b9 at the 7th fret – a shape you've played many times now. You should easily be able to work out the other chord shapes you need to visualise.

We lead into the first chord from the pickup bar. This hints at the original melody, which is notable for using a chromatic ascent up to a chord tone on beat 1. Here we anticipate the beat by targeting a D note (5th of G major). In bar one, we create a strong syncopation by playing notes on beats 2& and 4&. The notes are the root of the G major and the b7 of C7.

Visualising the "D" Shape CAGED voicing of G major in bar three, we begin a short ascending run that starts in bar two, anticipating the G chord. Notice here how adding a small articulation detail instantly makes the line more interesting. We're approaching the 3rd (B) of G major from a half step below with a legato slide.

In bar four, we leave an 1/8th note rest then descend chromatically to land on G#, the 3rd of E7b9, working around its 7th fret shape. Then we ascend in this shape up to an F on the second string – the b9.

From here, visualising an Am7 barre chord in 5th position, we can move into that shape with a half step movement from F to E, the 5th of Am7.

After playing two more notes in the Am7 shape, we begin to visualise the D7b9 in bar six in 5th position. We want to target the 3rd of this chord (F#), and this time we do so by switching position on the neck and climbing up to the 3rd chromatically from below on the fourth string. At the end of the D7 bar, notice that the final two notes ascend chromatically on the third string up to a B note, the 3rd of G major.

The 3rd interval is often the strongest way to move from chord to chord. In your next practice session, pick a favourite jazz standard and practice targeting the 3rd of each chord, using chromatic notes to move from one shape to the next. Think carefully about the lines you build – they've still got to be melodic!

Example 6b

This example uses the same G major and C7 shapes as the previous example. In bar one, you may notice that the Bb note at the end of the bar doesn't fit into the G shape – here we're just anticipating the C7 chord. The next couple of chord shapes are predictable, then we'll use the following voicings as our guide for bars 5-7

Am7   D7   G6/9

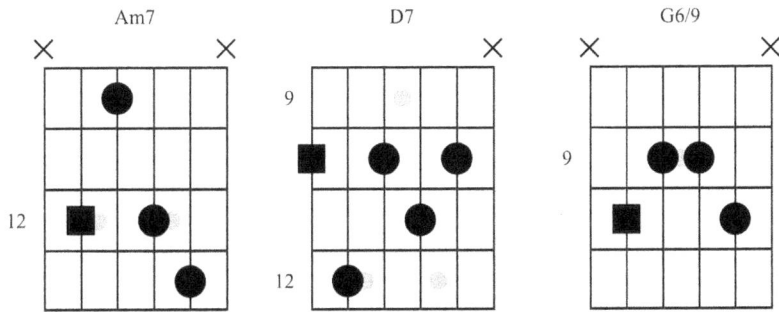

In bar one, this simple lick moves between the 5th and 6th of G major, implying a G6 harmony. At the end of the bar we play an early Bb note, which belongs to the C7 in bar two (the b7).

Bars 3-7 are another example of chord tone targeting with passing notes. We end the G major phrase on an A note (9th) and move down a half step to reach the 3rd (G#) of E7b9. Notice here the enclosure phrase over E7b9. The last three notes of the bar play a chromatic note above and below, followed by the E root note. Another enclosure idea in bar six helps us to highlight the 3rd (F#) of the D7 chord.

Example 6c

The next example moves through the series of guide chord shapes shown below. There are a couple of details to point out here.

In bar two, we could think in terms of either of the C#dim7 shapes below. Diminished 7 chords can be moved across the fretboard in minor 3rds (four frets including the starting fret) and each one will be an inversion of itself. These two shapes contain identical notes, just arranged in a different order.

For the B7b9 chord, as mentioned previously I usually play this voicing with my thumb over the neck for the bottom string, then my first and second fingers for the fourth and second strings. Finally, my third and fourth fingers fret the third and top strings.

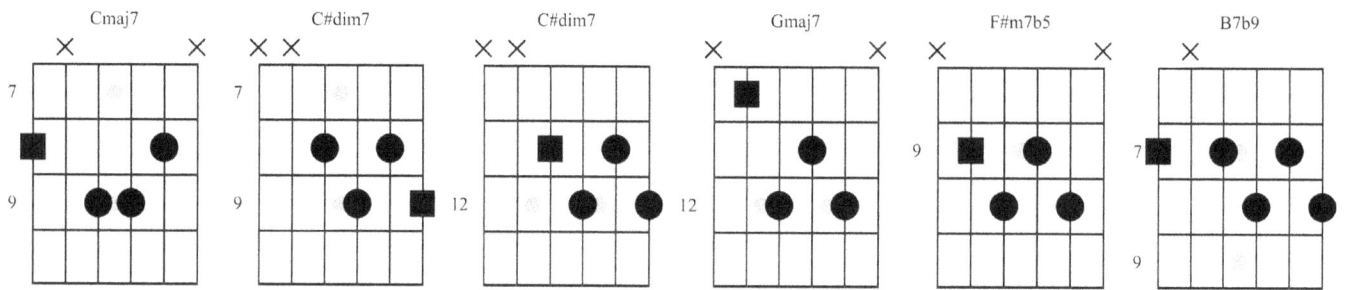

Cmaj7   C#dim7   C#dim7   Gmaj7   F#m7b5   B7b9

This section of the tune has some fast-moving chord changes and also switches emphasis from G Major to E Minor. This challenges us to create a melodic line that spells out the harmony, but still sounds melodic and not like a technical exercise!

We begin by chromatically descending to an F note, the b7 of G7. At the end of the pickup bar and bar one, you'll see that we play chord tones of Cmaj7 and C#dim7. In other words, we're signalling the chord change by playing a chord tone an 1/8th note before the chord is played.

The change from C#dim7 to Gmaj7 is made with a whole step movement on the top string, where we land on a D (5th of Gmaj7).

Next, we have a minor ii – V cadence: F#m7b5 – B7b9. Chromatically we descend to an E note, the b7 of the ii chord, then descend chromatically again to a D#, the 3rd of the V chord.

One tip here is that ii and V chords share several notes in common (F#m7b5 and B7b9 have three notes in common). Because of this, jazz musicians often simply this movement by just focusing on one or other of the chords. I.e., you could make B7b9 your focal point and the notes you play would still work over F#m7b5 or vice versa.

In bar five, we get to the Em7 chord via a half step movement on the top string, and the change to B7 is spelled out by playing a D# (3rd).

Example 6d

This line begins with an idea that shifts from a 5th position Am9 shape, into a 10th fret D7, to a 10th fret G6/9. After that, we play a short chord solo. As you work through the latter, remember that it's all about creating a melody, not just playing random chord voicings.

The tricky part about this line is the descending 1/8th note triplet lick, which needs some practice in order to play cleanly and evenly. We lead into it with a wide, sliding position shift, so it's a good idea to play the Am7 lick and the first part of the triplet lick in isolation – just to ensure you can change positions smoothly and get your fingers in the right place.

At the end of bar one, play the note on the 6th fret with your second finger, then slide it up to the 7th going into bar two. In bar two, your first finger will play the 5th fret on the first string, then you'll need to quickly slide the first finger up to the 10th fret to begin the descending triplet run.

Work out a fingering for the triplet run that you're comfortable with. I use my third finger quite a lot and favour small position changes, where others might stay in position and use their pinkie more. The best approach is the one that feels most natural to you.

Example 6e

In the next example, start by visualising the "D" Shape CAGED G major chord in 7th position shown earlier. From there, the line is built around the G6/9 and E7 shapes below. From bar five onwards we're thinking of a 12th fret Am7 shape into a 10th fret D7, then back up to the G6/9 shape.

Play this example through, thinking about the chord shapes as you go. Listen out for when you hit a chord tone that is important in spelling out the harmony. You are training your ears to separate chord tones from passing notes.

Example 6f

In bar one of the next example we can think of a G6 shape at the 12th fret. Barring the top four strings at the 12th gives us all four notes of the G6 chord, but to help you remember how to locate it, you can think of the low root note on the 5th string 10th fret, shown as a hollow square. Below we also have the shapes for the C7 and E7b9 chords. The rest are easy to work out!

The first few bars are built around a simple melodic motif that uses notes shared by G6 and C9 chords (the 9th is the D note at the end of bar two).

Take a closer look at bars 6-9 here, as it's a good example of the bebop language and echoes the kind of lines saxophonist Charlie Parker used to navigate chord changes – a mixture of chord tones and approach notes.

Example 6g

Here are the chord shapes to visualise for this next line.

We begin around a common Cmaj7 shape in the high register. Over the C#dim7 chord, we play a phrase that includes its root and b3, and targets the D note at the beginning of bar three, the 5th of G6.

In bars 4-5 the harmony focuses on different approaches to the B7 chord. To spell the change from F#m7b5 to B7, a chromatic run starts on F# and ends on D#, the 3rd of B7. Over the Em7 chord, this short phrase begins on E and ends on B. The B note is a chord tone of Em7 (5th) and the root of B7, then we further spell out the sound of B7 by playing its 3rd.

Example 6h

For the final part of the solo you can visualise the following sequence of shapes.

In this line you'll find more examples of chord tone targeting, but I want to draw your attention to the rhythmic variety.

Being able to weave around chord changes and spell out the harmony is a great skill to develop, but our lines will begin to sound a bit stale if we always play passages of straight 1/8th notes.

Here we mix up the note values so that certain phrases contain quicker and slower parts. In bars 1-3 you'll see a motif idea being developed, and we keep referring to those notes on the 8th/9th frets on the second and third strings. But it's the combination of 1/8th notes and 1/4 notes that make the line interesting.

In bars 4-6 we're playing mostly 1/8th notes, but introduce a couple of 1/8th note triplet phrases to break up the continuous 1/8th notes and create the impression that the line speeds up.

In bar seven, playing a quick 1/8th note followed by a dotted 1/4 note (the length of a 1/4 note and half its duration again) is another useful device to create some rhythmic variety.

Example 6i

When you're ready, have a go at working through the whole etude.

Example 6j – Full Solo

Cmaj7
C♯dim7
Gmaj7
F♯m7♭5
B7♭9
Em7
B7
Em7
A7
Am7
D7
G6
C7
Bm7
E7
Am7
D7
G6
Am7
D7
G6
C7
G
E7
TAB

Am7 D7 G6 Em7 Am7 D7
G6 C7 G6 E7♭9
Am7 D7 G6 G7
Cmaj7 C♯dim7 G6 F♯m7♭5 B7
Em7 B7 Em7 A7 Am7 D7

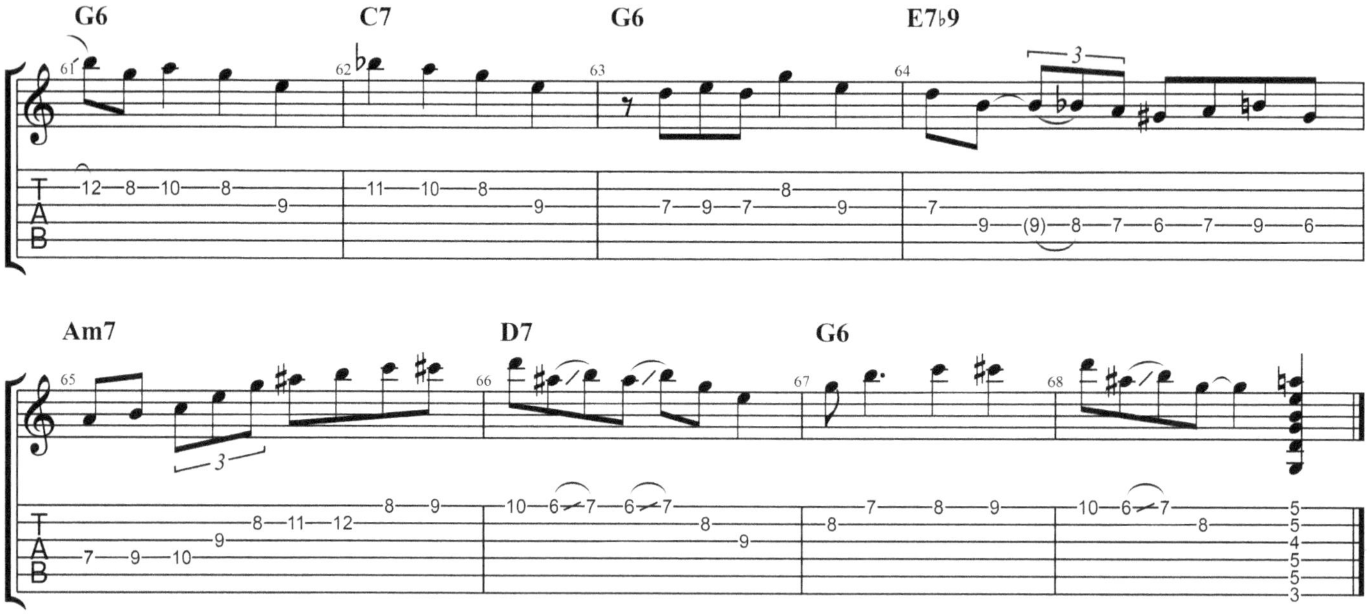
G6
C7
G6
E7♭9
Am7
D7
G6
T
A
B

Chapter Seven – Lulu Swing

Lulu Swing is a very popular jam session tune with a catchy melody, written by German jazz guitarist Häns'che Weiss and Romani guitarist Lulu Reinhardt. Both have significantly contributed to the Gypsy Jazz tradition.

The chord sequence in the A section is essentially a major key version of the sequence used in *Bossa Dorado's* A section. In fact, the A section melodies of these two tunes also have similarities in that they both feature a melodic motif that repeats itself while a note (in the lower register) descends in semitones to fit the chord changes.

Start by visualising this inversion of D6 at the 7th fret. Follow the chord shapes through to A7 and you'll work back to the D6 shape you began with.

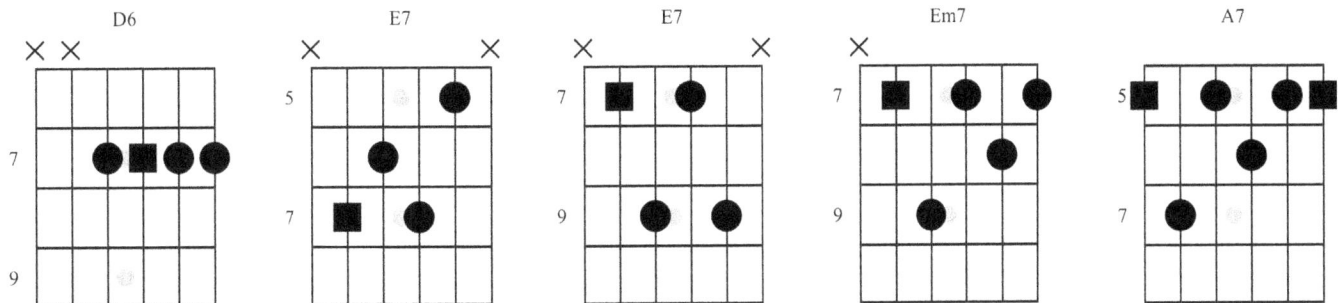

Lulu Swing is in the key of D Major and you'll notice in the first four bars that the chord changes go from D6 to E7. E7 doesn't belong to the key of D Major – rather it should be Em7 (as in bar five). This is a common harmonic movement in a number of jazz tunes (such as *Exactly Like You* and *Take the A Train*), so it's useful to learn how to navigate it.

Here, we play a motif phrase over D6, then land on G# (3rd of E7) on beat 1 of bar three. In bar four, we play an enclosure with a target note of E, beginning above it, then walking up to it chromatically from below.

The only difference between the chords E7 and Em7 is their 3rd (G# and G) respectively. So to play over the E7 to Em7 transition, we only have one note to worry about! At the end of bar five, the C# note doesn't belong to Em7 but is anticipating the A7 in bar six.

In bar seven, the A note we play as the chord changes from D6 to B7 is common to both chords, so we play a D# next (3rd of B7) to more clearly spell out the harmony.

Example 7a

In this example, in bar one we can think in terms of an open D major chord. For E7, it's a fifth string root, 7th position standard barre chord. The Em7 to A7 change also uses the expected chord shapes in 7th and 5th position respectively.

In bars 7-8, where we move from D to D7, this line can be seen as moving through the shapes below, from a D major triad to an inversion of D7.

In bars 1-4 we play a string-skipped motif. The melody notes that stand out (D and B, played firstly on the second string, then on the first string in the higher octave) work for both chords. In relation to D6 they are the root and 6th, and for E7 the b7 and 5th).

Bars 5-7 contain some chromatic movements to target chord tones. You should be very familiar with this approach now. See if you can spot the enclosure ideas here too.

Example 7b

Remember that diminished 7 chords can be moved across the fretboard in minor 3rds (four frets including the starting note). In 12th position we get this inversion with the root note on the third string.

This melodic idea is formed around three voicings that are close together. Think of a 10th fret, fifth string root Gmaj7, followed by the diminished 7 shape above, then a 10th fret, sixth string root D6.

Working with just the top two strings in bars 1-2, this lick focuses on highlighting the difference between the Gmaj7 and G#dim7 chords. They share two notes in common and have two notes different. G#dim7 has an F compared to Gmaj7's F#, and we can use this to distinguish between the chords without having to play the obvious root note.

In bar three, we weave around the 10th fret D7 shape and land on the chord's 3rd (F#) on beat 4.

Example 7c

Next, think of a 7th position E7 chord for bars 1-3. We're using chromatic passing notes in this line to target the 3rd (G#) of the E7 chord at the beginning of bar three. In bar three, the idea is built around a 7th position Em7 shape. For the A7, you can visualise this A13 shape.

A13

Example 7d

In bar two of this example, start by visualising the simple 7th fret D6 shape on the top four strings shown in Example 7b. In bar three, we play the nearby root of the E7 chord on the 9th fret. Work out the other shapes being used to create the melodic line – they are all pretty intuitive.

In bar one, the melodic line spells out the chord with chord tones falling on every down-beat. We spell out the E7 harmony in bar three by playing the root note, then slide into the higher position from the 3rd.

In bars five and six, notice how we use descending and ascending chromatic notes to target Em7 and A7 chord tones. Some rhythmic variety is built into the final three bars to keep things interesting, and there are more descending chromatic phrases in bars 7-8.

Example 7e

Here is another long line, which moves through several different chord shapes in the higher register. Some are probably shapes you don't often reach for, so I'll spell them all out for you. Familiarise yourself with the shapes by playing through them a few times, so you can visualise them when learning the melodic line.

The simple opening phrase suggests a Dmaj9 harmony by playing the 3rd, root, 9th and back to the root. In bar two, a little tension is introduced by playing an F note before resolving to F# (3rd). You can make a simple idea like this work harder by using rhythmic variety. For example, all the notes in bar one are played on the down-beats, while in bar two the first three notes are all on the off-beats. The final note in bar two is played on beat 4 but tied across the bar line into bar three.

Bars 5-8 show another example of weaving through the chord tones using mostly 1/8th notes. Do some analysis of your own on this line. First identify the chord tones, then consider how we're approaching them. Next, think about how we're connecting one chord to the next.

When playing this line, focus on getting the most out of the articulation by smoothly executing the legato slides and hammer-ons/pull-offs.

Example 7f

The shapes to visualise should be self-explanatory in this example. There's nothing unusual, so work through it and map out the chord shapes to work around.

We start here with a bouncing rhythmic line that highlights a D note – the 5th of both chords in bars 1-2. In bar three, the emphasis is on an E, the 9th of the D major chord.

In bar five, a descending chromatic phrase targets the root of the E7. In bar six, this phrase outlines an E9 chord. In bar seven we use an enclosure phrase to target the 3rd (F#) of D major, then ascend to drop onto a C note over D7 (the b7).

Example 7g

Think around these two shapes for G#dim7 in bar two of the next example.

The opening phrase over G major sets up a diminished arpeggio sequence over the G#dim7 chord, which launches from a half step below the root note at the end of bar one. The rest of the line is based on a motif idea, where D and F# notes are repeated throughout. Over D major in bars 3-4, those notes are the root and 3rd. Over the E7 bars that follow, they are the b7 and 5th.

When we change chord to Em7 in bar seven, these notes represent the b7 and 9th. Because we're creating a melody from just a couple of notes, notice that in bars five and seven the line is punctuated with chord stabs that highlight the change from E7 to Em7. In fact, over the Em7 bar, the two notes used imply the sound of an Em7b5, so that bars 7-8 sound like a minor ii – V cadence.

Example 7h

This final example uses a repeating lick on the second and third string to propel the solo to its climax. Pay close attention to how the line is articulated. Although we use the same notes on the third string throughout, we alternate between picking the 10th fret and sliding into the 11th fret, and picking both notes individually. In terms of note choice, we're sliding into the 3rd (F#) and bouncing off the 5th (A) on the second string.

In bars 4-5 we need to adapt the lick slightly to accommodate the E7 chord. We keep the F# note, which is the 9th of E7, and lower the A note to G# on the second string – the 3rd of E7.

The rest of the line weaves around the chord tones (a concept you should feel much more comfortable with now) and ends with a D major triad inversion.

Example 7i

Work through the whole solo slowly and try to commit as much of it as you can to memory. Also pick out your favourite licks and ideas from the solo and use them to jam over the backing track, adding your own ideas.

Example 7j – Full Solo

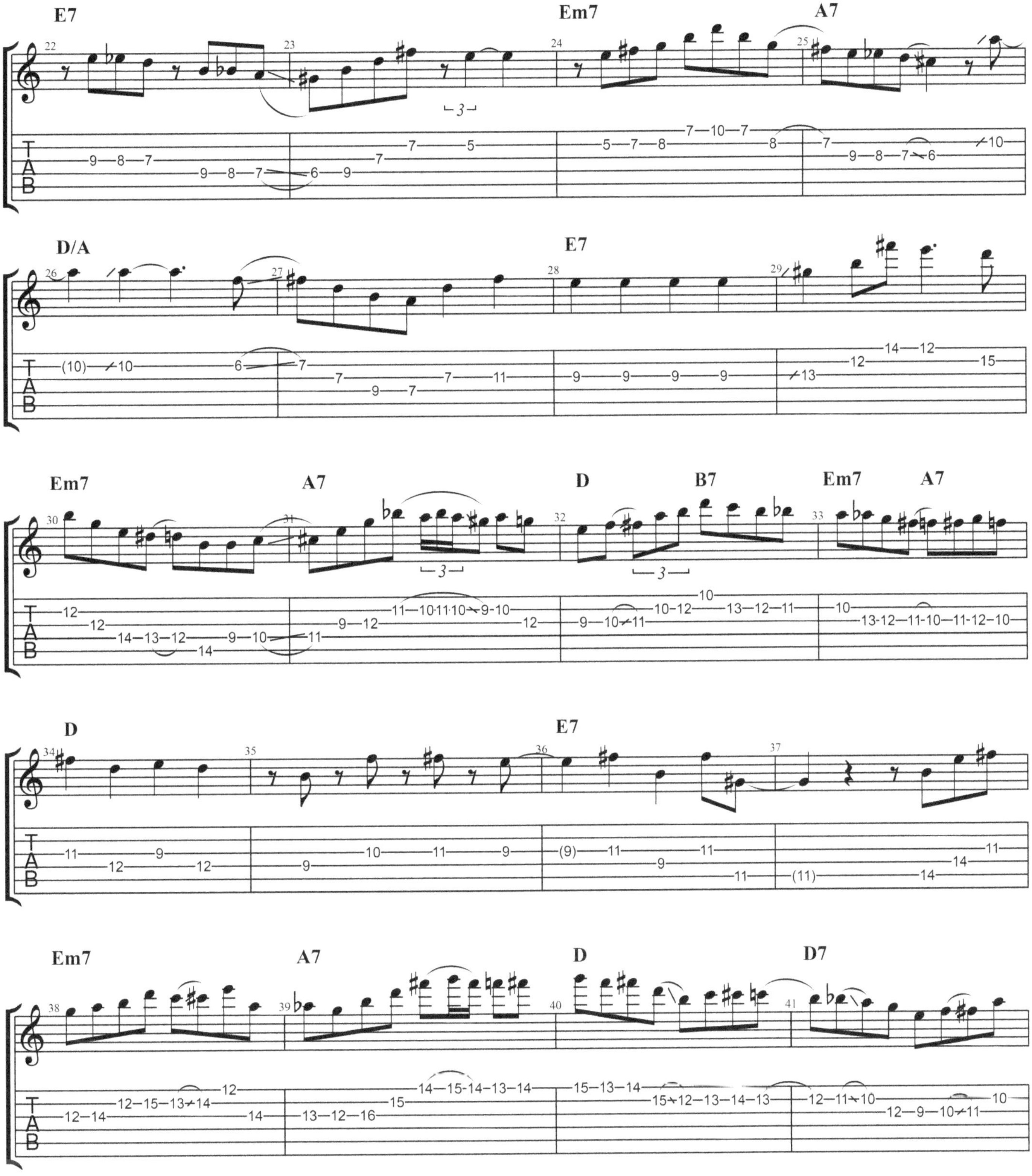
E7
Em7
A7
D/A
E7
Em7
A7
D
B7
Em7
A7
D
E7
Em7
A7
D
D7

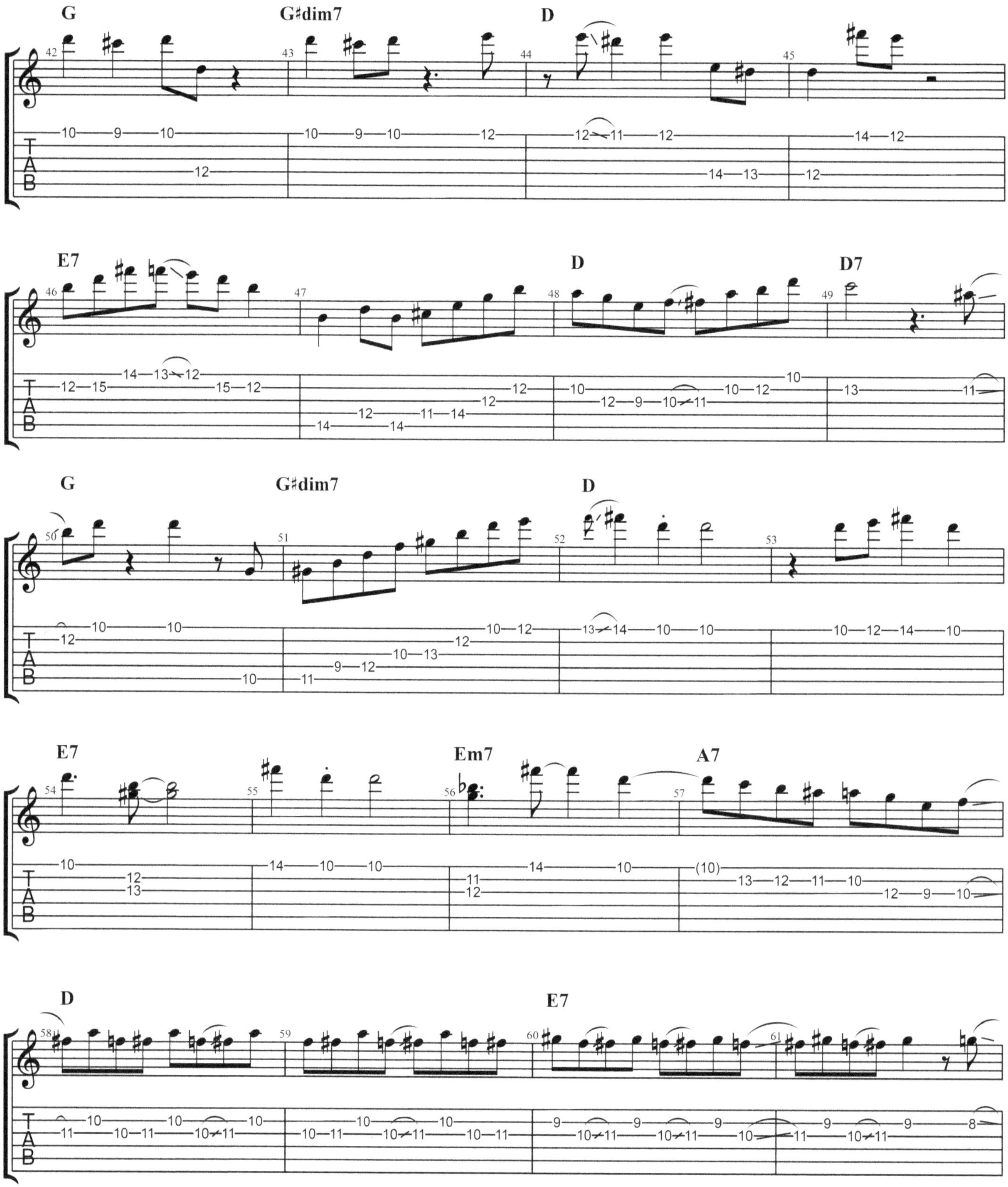
G
G♯dim7
D
E7
D
D7
G
G♯dim7
D
E7
Em7
A7
D
E7
TAB

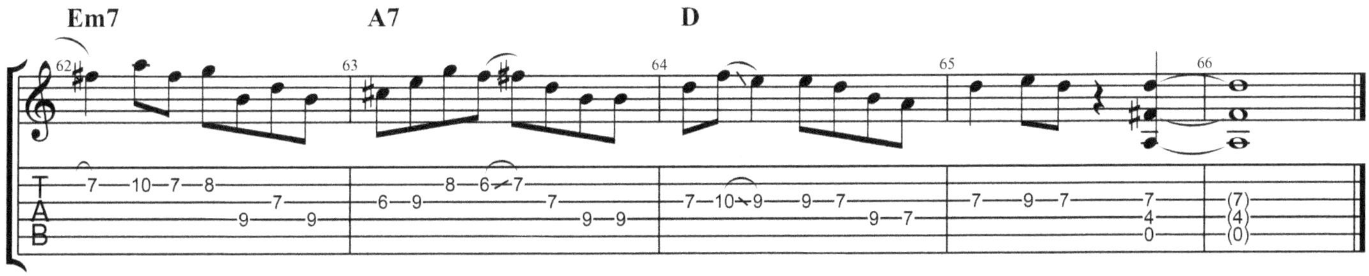
Em7
A7
D
62
63
64
65
66
T
A
B

Conclusion

I hope you've enjoyed this third outing of Gypsy Jazz etudes. As well as learning some useful vocabulary, I hope you'll be inspired to write your own licks. Throughout the book you've had lots of practice at visualising chord shapes and seeing how melodic lines can be constructed around them. Take this idea into your practice times and explore it more deeply. You've also refined your understanding of chord tone soloing, adding chromaticism and rhythmic variation. To become more fluent with these skills, here's a suggested practice routine you can follow:

Warm-Up (10-15 mins)

- **Chord Tone Visualisation**: Pick a chord (e.g., Dm7) and map out its chord tones across the fretboard

- **Enclosure Drills**: Practice enclosures by targeting a chord tone with notes above and below

- **Chromatic Runs**: Play simple licks using chromatic passing notes, emphasising the down-beats of each bar with chord tones

Etude Breakdown (20-30 mins)

Choose one solo from the book.

- **Loop 2–4 bars** at a time. Identify the chords being outlined and the shapes used

- **Analyse** how chromaticism and rhythmic phrasing have been applied

- **Play slowly**, ensuring your phrasing is clean and articulate

Lick Repurposing (15 mins)

Isolate a favourite lick from the etudes.

- **Transpose it** to different keys

- **Play it** in different octaves

- **Apply it** over similar progressions (e.g., minor blues or Rhythm Changes) to hear what effect it has

Improvisation Practice (15-20 mins)

Jam over the book's backing tracks.

- Use one chord shape or one technique at a time (e.g., guide tones, diminished arpeggios)

- Experiment with rhythmic displacement and motif development

Weekly Focus Areas

Pick one area per week to work on

- **Week 1-2**: Minor Blues Soloing – work through both G Minor blues etudes

- **Week 3-4**: Rhythmic Variation – focus on *Lady Be Good* and *Lulu Swing*

- **Week 5-6**: Diminished Concepts & Enclosures – work on *Joseph Joseph* and *Bossa Dorado*

- **Week 7-8:** Work on developing your chord soloing skills by experimenting with voicings arranged on the top four strings

Keep listening to the greats of Gypsy Jazz guitar and seek out recordings that inspire you. The more you internalise the sound of this joyful music, the more it will surprise you by coming out in your playing.

Make sure to have fun with it – there's always more to explore!

Remi

www.ingramcontent.com/pod-product-compliance
Lightning Source LLC
Chambersburg PA
CBHW081434090426
42740CB00017B/3295